The California Wine Country
Herbs & Spices Cookbook
The Revised Second Edition

Compiled and Edited
by
Virginia and Robert Hoffman

Authors of:
The California Wine Country Cookbooks, I & II
The California Wine Country Herbs & Spices Cookbook
The Great Turkey Cookbook & CD-ROM
The Great Chicken Cookbook
The Holidays Cookbook
Salsas!
Cooking With Wine
Good Taste Begins with B & G
The Great Little Food With Wine Cookbook

The Hoffman Press
Santa Rosa, California

Quantity discounts and bulk purchases of this and other Hoffman Press books are available. Call or fax the National Sales Manager at (707) 538-5527, Fax (707) 538-7371.

Cover: "Golden Vineyard Hills of California" by Ellie Marshall
Drawings from "The Spice Cookbook," © 1964, 1991. All rights reserved.
Published by David White Company, Willsboro, NY 12996. Used with permission. Typeset by Nancy LaMothe

Publisher's Cataloging-in-Publication
(Provided by Quality Books, Inc.)

The California wine country herb & spices cookbook : 96 wine
    country chefs share 212 of their best herbs and spices
    recipes / compiled and edited by Virginia & Robert Hoffman.
    -- 2nd ed., rev. -- Santa Rosa, CA : Hoffman Press, c1998
        p. cm.
        Included index.

        1. Cookery (Herbs) 2. Cookery (Spices) 3. Cookery
(Wine) 4. Cookery, American--California style. I.
Hoffman, Virginia. II. Hoffman, Robert. III. Title: Herbs
& spices cookbook IV. Title: Herbs and spices cookbook

TX819.H4C34 1998   641.6'57
                              QBI98-273

The Cuisine of the California Wine Country

"The California Wine Country has become a center of creative cuisine, thanks to the chefs of the wineries, the culinary schools, the restaurants, and the residents of this region."

When we wrote those words in 1994 in the preface to the first "California Wine Country Herbs & Spices Cookbook," we had no idea that this cuisine would become so popular throughout the world so quickly.

This cuisine is best described as "the usage of common and uncommon ingredients in the preparation of traditional and non-traditional dishes." In the field of herbs and spices it has resulted in some truly outstanding recipes. Basil, for example, has been a basic ingredient in pastas and pizzas for hundreds of years. Now, try a pinch of basil when cooking green vegetables.

Another example would be cinnamon, a spice traditionally associated with pumpkin pies and cinnamon toast. When you add it to mashed potatoes or to a beef stew, you're participating in California Wine Country cuisine!

We hope that this book encourages you to try different herbs and spices with different foods. We want you to say: "I wonder how this would taste with this spice instead of the one I have always used?" Use this book as the base for your entry into a whole new world of cookery.

Besides the recipes by these great chefs, we have included recipes for making herbed and spiced butters, vinegars and oils, and how to make spice mixes to suit your taste (and budget).

We hope that the use of this book gives you as much pleasure as publishing it gave to us.

Virginia and Robert Hoffman
Santa Rosa, California, 1998

The Table of Contents

An Introduction 3

Contributors 7

History of Herbs and Spices 9

Herbs & Spices and What To Do With Them 13

Appetizers & Light Foods 29

Soups 49

Salads 67

Pastas & Grains 87

Meats 105

Poultry 129

Seafood 147

Vegetables 165

Desserts 177

Salsas, Sauces and Condiments 201

Herbed Butters 215

Herbed Vinegars & Oils 219

Herb and Spice Mixes 230

Index of Recipes 234

Postscript 239

Contributors

We are indebted to two people who contribute substantially to our books: Nancy LaMothe, who structures our recipes (this is her tenth book with us) and Ellie Marshall, the distinguished artist, who illustrates our covers.

We want to convey our appreciation to the wineries of The California Wine Country for their generosity in sharing their best recipes featuring herbs and spices. It was a difficult task to determine which were the best of the many that we received. We think you'll agree when you make them.

A word of explanation: Because each chef has his or her own way of writing a recipe, it is often difficult for the reader to follow the recipes. We have reformatted all the recipes in this book to provide the ingredients in the order in which they are used. When ingredients have been used that are available only in the local region of the chef, we have substituted ingredients that are more widely available in supermarkets and gourmet stores, nationally.

Many of the recipe names have been changed from the original ones used, due to duplication or similarity. We have not attributed specific recipes to specific wineries because there was considerable duplication of recipes.

But, they have all been tested. They are all good. And we think you'll agree with us, when we say, "Here's a taste of the California Wine Country."

Adler Fels Winery, Alderbrook Vineyards, Arrowood Vineyards & Winery, Beaucanon Winery, Benziger Family Winery, Bergfeld Winery, Beringer Vineyards, Buena Vista Carneros Winery, Cakebread Cellars, Canandaigua Wine Co., Carneros Alambic Distillery, Carneros Estate, Charles Spinetta Winery and Gallery, Chateau St. Jean, Chateau Souverain, Cline Cellars, Concannon Vineyards, Conn Creek Winery, Cordoniu Napa, De Loach Vineyards, Domaine Carneros, Domaine Chandon, Dry Creek Vineyards, Duckhorn Vineyards, Dunnewood Vineyards and Winery, Eberle Winery, Edgewood Estate, Ferrari-Carano Vineyards and Winery, Fess Parker Winery, Fetzer Vineyards, Franciscan Oakville Estate, Freemark Abbey Vineyard, Freixenet Sonoma Champagne Caves.

Contributors

Glen Ellen Vineyards & Winery, Gloria Ferrer Champagne Caves, Granite Springs Winery, Heitz Wine Cellars, Heublein Inc, Inglenook-Napa Valley, Jordon Vineyards and Winery, Kendall-Jackson Vineyards, Kenwood Vineyards, Konocti Winery, Korbel Champagne Cellars, Kunde Estate Winery, Lake Sonoma Winery, Lambert Bridge, Landmark Vineyards, J. Lohr Winery & Vineyards, Louis M. Martini Winery, Mark West Vineyards, Markham Winery, Martinl & Prati Winery, Matanzas Creek Winery, Merryvale Vineyards, Mirassou, Monterey Vineyards, Montevina Winery, Monticello Cellars, Mumm Cuvée Napa, Murphy-Goode Estate Winery, J. Pedroncelli Winery, Peju Province, Quivera Vineyards, Ravenswood, Raymond Vineyard & Cellar, Robert Mondavi Winery, Robert Stemmler Vineyards, Rodney Strong Vineyards, Round Hill Vineyards, Russian River Vineyards & Restaurant, Rutherford Hill Winery, V. Sattui Winery, Sausal Winery, Scharffenberger Cellars, Schug Carneros Estate Winery, Simi Winery, Inc., Smothers Bros Winery, Sonoma Mission Inn and Spa, St. Supery Vineyards & Winery, St. Francis Winery, Stag's Leap Cellars, Sterling Vineyards, Sutter Home Winery, Taylor Wine Co., Torres Vineyard & Winery, Viansa Winery, Wente Bros. Wine Cellars, Whitehall Lane Winery, Windsor Vineyards and Winery.

A note about the wine suggestions: Many of the appetizers, soups, salads and desserts have wine suggestions. We do not suggest that you must serve four or five different wines with a meal. They are there if you serve that particular dish alone, such as a soup or a salad served as a light meal.

Generally, the wine you choose for your main course is served for the entire meal. We do suggest, however, that the wines suggested for the desserts are worthy of special consideration when you are having a special dinner or luncheon for special family or friends.

VMH & RPH

Herbs
&
Spices

THE HERBS & SPICES COOKBOOK

A Brief History of Herbs and Spices

Archeologists tell us that primitive man was using spices as early as 50,000 B.C. It is believed that it probably started when he wrapped his meat in some leaves to keep the dirt and ashes off while cooking and discovered that the meat tasted better. At that moment, mankind discovered the art of seasoning.

The history of spices has been chronicled on the walls of the Egyptian pyramids and the scripture of the Bible. Joseph, of the coat of many colors, was sold to spice traders by his envious older brother, "And behold, a company of Ishmaelites came from Gilead with their camels bearing spicery and balm and myrrh, going to carry it down to Egypt."

In those times, caravans of as many as 4,000 camels carrying spices made the long perilous journey from the East to Rome, Carthage, Alexandria and other cities in Nineveh and Babylon where the spices were sold. This was "The Golden Road to Samarkand".

For centuries the Arabs controlled all of the spice trade. They achieved this by keeping their sources a secret. It was not until the chronicles of Marco Polo's travels, in the late 1200's, that the trade door was opened to the Far East when he reported where the spices came from and how they could be exported.

As European traders realized that they could invade this very profitable market, they outfitted ships for the spice trade. Christopher Columbus and Ferdinand Magellan were two of the many explorers seeking ship routes to the Orient.

Spain, Portugal, Holland, France, and England all joined the fray, and in the process, colonized many spice growing countries to control the export of their spices. Sumatra, Ceylon, Java, India and Malacca all came under foreign rule for their spices.

Gradually, by war with each other and conquest of spice growing nations, England became the most dominant spice trader in the world. This continued until America entered the spice trade and broke the monopoly with fast sailing ships which brought spices from the Far East to the New World.

Today, America is the largest importer and consumer of spices in the world.

While most spices are imported, more than 200,000 pounds of spices are grown in the United States each year, with California as the major producer. American-grown herbs and spices include capsicum peppers, paprika, basil, tarragon, mint, parsley, sage, and marjoram, and seeds such as mustard, dill, fennel, and sesame.

Now, on to the herbs and spices, and what to do with them.

Herbs and Spices
And What To Do With Them

ALLSPICE
Originally from Jamaica, it got its name from the aroma which suggests a blend of cloves, cinnamon and nutmeg. Some places, such as the West Indies, still call it "pimento," the original Spanish name.

It is available in whole berries or ground. Use the whole berries to season gravies, broths, and pickling. Use the ground in making bouillabaisse, chowder, and in steaming fresh fish.

ANISE SEED
A medicine in ancient Assyria, it was used as a digestive at Roman banquets, and considered a charm against "the evil eye" in olden times. This seed of the celery family has a distinctive licorice taste. Used widely in baking cookies and cakes, and when added to fruit compotes, it is also an excellent spice for chicken, duck, and veal dishes. Originally from the eastern Mediterranean region, it is now grown in Turkey and Spain.

STAR ANISE
Despite having a similar name to anise seed, star anise is from a different plant. It is the hard brown fruit of an evergreen tree in China which dries in the shape of a star. The flavor, however, is licorice, like anise seed and can be used in the same manner as anise seed.

BASIL

A native of India and Persia, this member of the mint family is rich in folklore. Hindus plant it around their homes and temples to insure happiness. In France it is called "Herbe Royale" because it is so important to French cuisine. In Italy, young Italians wear a sprig of it to indicate that they are in love.

Basil is best known for seasoning pizza, spaghetti sauces and tomato dishes. It adds a wonderful aroma to all kinds of cooked vegetables. It is also an important ingredient in the making of Chartreuse and other liqueurs. It is now grown in the United States, Egypt and France.

BAY LEAVES

The legend says that a beautiful nymph was fleeing from Apollo, the Greek god. The gods turned her into an evergreen tree whose leaves were to become the symbol of victory and scholarship. The tree is known today as the laurel or sweet-bay tree.

Our word for a college graduate "Baccalaureate" comes from "laurel berries" and "winning your laurels". The appropriate saying for this spice is "To win a laurel wreath for your brow, put a laurel leaf in the stew pot now."

A large leaf, about 2 to 3 inches long, it should be used sparingly. One or two leaves will suffice. Unique and really good with stews, soups and sauces, bay leaves are mainly available only in the whole leaf form. They come from Turkey and Greece.

CARAWAY SEEDS

This aromatic spice was introduced into the western world when Roman legions, 2000 years ago, brought it to England. It was ground as flour to bake bread, the oil was used for cooking, and the whole seed for flavoring.

It is widely used throughout the world in bread making and in making cheese. Try it on pork and sauerkraut dishes, soups, meats, and stews. Sprinkle it on cottage cheese, coleslaw and potato salad. It is also the principal ingredient in the making of Kümmel cordial.

CARDAMOM

It has such diverse uses, it is difficult to say what it should be used for. The Vikings brought cardamom to Scandinavia, where it is used in practically all baked goods. In India it is essential in the making of curry. In the Middle East it is used in coffee. In other parts of the world it is used in making pickles, frankfurters, and coffee cake. It is the key ingredient in "Old Bay Seasoning", a blend of herbs and spices used in making seafood ragouts and gumbos.

CAYENNE AND CHILE PEPPER

Originating in the Caribbean, they were first identified in the annals of Christopher Columbus. Actually, they are not peppers, but chilies called capsicum, with vast differences in their hot, peppery flavors.

Cayenne is one of the hottest, and is used in the making of chili con carne, barbecue sauces, and similar foods of Latin America. Chili powder is usually a blend of different chilies to produce a warm and soothing flavor without the harshness of pure cayenne pepper. Use the powder in baking fish. Dust it over tomato and mushroom soups.

CELERY SEED

It really isn't the seed of the celery; it is the seed of the smallage plant, a distant wild relative of celery. It has a warm, slightly bitter celery taste.

One of the oldest spices known to man and used as a medicine for hundreds of years, it is so small that it takes nearly 750,000 seeds to make one pound! Imported from India and China, it is available in both seed and ground forms.

Note: Don't confuse pure celery seed with celery salt. Celery salt is a blend of table salt with celery seed and is quite different in its application. If you are preparing a low-salt dish, do not use celery salt. Both are good with fish, soups, potato salad, salad dressings, and croquettes.

CHERVIL

This member of the parsley family has been in use as a seasoning since it came to Rome 2,000 years ago with Roman legions returning from eastern Europe and Asia. Chervil leaves are used as an alternative to parsley, but is more like tarragon in aroma and flavor.

Although it is used in omelettes, salads, stuffings and sauces, its principal use is as an ingredient in the blend "Fines Herbes". Sold in whole form, it is imported from France and is also now grown in the United States.

CHILI POWDER (See HERB & SPICE MIXES)

CHIVES
If it were not for flash freezing, most of us would never know the pleasure of using this aromatic member of the onion family in dried form.

Chives have unlimited uses. The classic, of course, is baked potatoes with sour cream and chives, but don't restrict yourself to that. Add chives to all cooked green vegetables and green salads, cream sauces, gravies, and dips.

Grown and produced in the United States, they are available fresh, frozen and flash-frozen dried.

CINNAMON
Cinnamon is one of the first spices used and enjoyed by man. It was used as a flavoring for food, a medicine, a perfume, and burned as incense; and, it was an important ingredient of "Love Potions" in early times.

This spice comes from the dried bark of an evergreen tree that is peeled, and rolled into long sticks called "quills".

Available in both the stick and ground form, it is one of our most important baking spices in the ground form, while the stick form is used in pickling spices, making sugar syrups, and in beef stews. Hot chocolate with a cinnamon stick is a gourmet-grade beverage, particularly on a cold, snowy day.

CLOVES
In the Moluccas, where cloves were first discovered, a clove tree was planted when a child was born. Despite this peaceful beginning, bloody wars were fought for the possession of this versatile spice. Today, cloves are grown in Madagascar, Brazil and Zanzibar.

Available both whole and ground, the whole clove is used in studding ham and pork, in meat stews and gravies, and in pickling. Ground cloves bring out wonderful flavors in baked goods, puddings, chocolate in any form, and when sprinkled on winter squash.

CORIANDER SEED
A native of the Mediterranean, this spice goes back 3,000 years for its first known usage of adding fragrance to the Hanging Gardens of Babylon.

Leaves of this plant are commonly called "cilantro" and "Chinese parsley."

This mild, delicately-fragrant spice is used in the ground form as a baking spice for pastries, cookies and cakes. In the whole or seed form, it is the most important ingredient in curries, pickling spices, and in frankfurters.

CUMIN SEED
This is another spice that predates Biblical times. In Mathew 23, Jesus says "...ye pay tithe of Mint and Anise and Cumin".

Many superstitions are associated with cumin. A happy life awaited the bride and groom who carried cumin in the wedding ceremony. If the seed was cursed when it was planted, it would produce a wonderful crop.

A native of Egypt, it is processed in the whole seed form and ground. It is an important ingredient in chili powder and curry powder. In Germany it is used with pork and sauerkraut, and the Dutch and Swiss like to add it to cheeses.

DILL SEED/WEED

Once thought to be a deterrent to witches, it was also prescribed in ancient times as a nerve-calming tea.

The seed is the dried fruit of a plant in the parsley family. The weed is made from the leaves. Grown widely in Europe, it is now grown in the United States and India.

Both are sold, mainly, in the whole form. Dill seed is essential in making dill pickles, and is excellent in meats, fish, sauces, salads, coleslaw, potato salad, macaroni, and in sauerkraut. Dill weed is suited to salads, sandwich fillings and boiled fish dishes.

FENNEL SEED

Once considered an aphrodisiac, an aid to weight loss, and a cure for loss of vision, this spice has become an important element in the cuisine of Italy. Pasta sauces, breads and sausage making are the key usages of this spice. Use it, too, in seafood, pork and poultry dishes.

FENUGREEK SEED

This little known spice was originally used as a stimulator for the digestive processes, and as fodder for cattle. It was also water-soaked to make a paste to decrease fevers in humans. The very small reddish brown seeds have a pleasantly bitter flavor, and are an important part of curry powder and chutneys. An unusual use is in the making of imitation maple flavoring!

19

GARLIC
Purists claim that it is not a spice but a vegetable, but we have it here because it is probably the single most-used flavoring agent in America today.

While garlic is centuries old in its usage in Europe and the Middle and Far East, America used a minimal amount of it until the return of soldiers from Europe and the East at the close of World War II.

Available fresh, frozen, freeze-dried, dried, and in powder, it is used in nearly everything. For something new, put a dusting of garlic powder on steamed vegetables, and just before you serve tomato, navy bean, or split pea soup.

GINGER
The favorite spice of one of the authors of this book, ginger has a multitude of uses. Ginger was one of the first true Oriental spices to come to the West from Asia.

For centuries, it was the rich-man's spice, rivaling black pepper in price. Gingerbread was in existence in Greece almost 5,000 years ago. The Norman conquest of England brought ginger there, where it soon became the prized spice of royalty. It was brought to the Caribbean by Spanish explorers, and then to the United States by natives emigrating here.

Ginger is available whole, cracked, ground, crystallized, and preserved.

Common uses of ginger are in baking, making pickling spice, and ginger ale. We suggest you do as we do — rub it sparingly into meat, fowl and fish. And, for something truly special, use crystallized ginger when baking apples or serving vanilla ice cream.

LAVENDER
This aromatic herb is just beginning to be appreciated as a culinary ingredient and not simply as a perfume for soaps, etc. From the Mediterranean originally, it is usually associated with England, where it has been popular for many centuries. It came to America with the Pilgrims and has flourished here ever since.

Lavender is available as fresh leaves and flowers, and as dried flowers. (It is safer to use commercially grown lavender that is free from insecticides and pesticides.)

It is very pungent, so use it sparingly on meat such as roast lamb, vegetables, salads, and fruits preserved in syrup.

MARJORAM
A member of the mint family, and also related to oregano, it is a great asset in the kitchen. Originally considered the herb of happiness, wreaths of it were worn by the bride and groom.

Marjoram is wonderful in the making of split pea soup, poultry dressing, meat stew, salad dressings, and seafood sauces.

MINT
It has been a symbol of hospitality for centuries before the mint julep was invented in Kentucky! The ancients used it "in chambers and places of recreation, repose and pleasure."

Available as flakes or leaves, it is widely used for candies, frozen desserts, chocolate dishes, salads, and cooked peas and carrots.

Mint jelly and mint sauce are famous accompaniments for roast or barbecued lamb. We use it, too, as a dusting on new potatoes, carrots and peas, and in making mint vinegar salad dressing.

MUSTARD

Anatole France wrote: "A tale without love is like beef without mustard: an insipid dish." Millions of people must agree with this because it takes a crop of more than 400 million pounds a year to satisfy the demand.

It is unique in the fact that, when dry it has no aroma or flavor, but when dampened it develops its characteristic odor and bite in 10 to 15 minutes.

Available as whole seed, powdered, or prepared as a paste, it is an enhancer of meats, fish, fowl, sauces, salad dressings, cheese and egg dishes. The seeds are used in pickling, with boiled beets, and as a garnish on salads.

NUTMEG AND MACE

While nutmeg and mace come from the same tree, they are quite different in their usages. Nutmeg is the heart of the fruit, mace is made from the fleshy meat around the fruit. Nutmeg is sweeter, more pungent and has a very distinctive aroma. Mace is stronger and coarser. Both are available in ground form, but only nutmeg is available in the whole form. To enjoy the ultimate flavor of nutmeg, buy it whole and grate it as you need it.

Both are so versatile that they are essential components in cakes, puddings, meats, vegetables, pastas, and even fruit dishes. Try it in chicken soup, herbed butter, and in candied sweet potatoes.

ONION

Yes, you are right, that onions are not herbs or spices, but we put it in this list because they should be here. Onions contribute so much flavor to food! They are available fresh, dried in flakes, minced and as onion salt. (Warning: Onion salt is table salt mixed with dehydrated onion. Don't use it in salt-restricted diets.)

OREGANO

In the United States, oregano owes its fame to pizza, and pizza came to the U.S. when servicemen, returning from World War II in Italy raved about "the tomato pies" they had there. In just a few years pizza had become an American staple and chefs were finding new uses for oregano, this new, yet centuries-old spice.

Another type of oregano is used in Mexican and Latin-American dishes. Available both whole and ground, it is ideal when cooking tomatoes, zucchini or green beans. When barbecuing meat, fish or poultry, put a bunch or two of fresh oregano on the coals.

PAPRIKA

The sweetish, mild odor and taste of paprika is only part of its attributes, as it adds a rich reddish color to the foods in which it is used. Known for its usage in chili con carne and goulash, it is also an excellent ingredient in making stews, vegetable soups, and as a garnish on casserole dishes and cottage cheese. A plus is the fact that it is a wonderful breath freshener, too.

PARSLEY

Parsley is best known as the principal ingredient in French cuisine by its presence in "Bouquet Garni" and "Fines Herbes," the former being mixed into dishes such as quiche, and the latter being the little bag of herbs and spices suspended into the cooking dish and removed prior to serving.

Its mild flavor goes well with poultry, fish and egg dishes. Use it as a garnish in salad dressing, casserole dishes, cottage cheese and soups. You may choose to use a sprig to decorate your plate. It is particularly useful as a breath freshener too.

PEPPER

Pepper is one of the oldest seasonings known to man. Both black and white pepper come from the berries of the same vine. The black is from the berries before they mature, the white from the fully ripened berries.

Both are available in whole, medium and coarse ground. For the best flavor, use the whole and grind it yourself. Remember that black pepper is more pungent than white, but white pepper is far hotter. When recipes call for "pepper" it means black pepper unless the recipe specifically calls for white pepper.

POPPY SEEDS

While they come from the same plant that produces opium, there is no problem of addiction as the seeds are formed after the plant loses its opium producing qualities. Although it takes 900,000 to make a pound, these tiny seeds are very flavorful.

Use them in sauces for pasta, rice, new potatoes, boiled onions, broiled fish, and on any green vegetable.

ROSEMARY
Known for its delicate fragrance, it was immortalized in Shakespeare's Hamlet by Ophelia "...There's rosemary, that's for remembrance." Used since time immemorial as the wreath for brides, it has a fresh bittersweet taste that goes well with lamb, chicken, and seafood. Use it sparingly, as it can dominate a dish!

SAFFRON
Saffron, the world's most expensive spice, is also one of the most potent. Only a few strands will flavor and color large quantities of a dish. It is essential in the making of the Spanish dish paella, and in Moroccan couscous. If you prefer to start with something simpler, use just two or three strands in boiling water when cooking four to six portions of rice, and you will have a rich, golden rice with a delicate, exotic flavor.

SAGE
Medieval herbalists believed that sage improved the memory and insured long life. Since colonial times in America, it has been considered an essential seasoning, particularly for split-pea soup, poultry stuffings, pork dishes, salad dressings and chowders.

Sage is available in whole, ground, or rubbed form. (Rubbed sage is fluffy and imparts better flavor.) Make your own croutons for salads and soups by dusting sage on cubed bread before toasting.

SAVORY
There are two savories: Summer and Winter. The Summer is the milder of the two and the more useful as it does not tend to dominate a dish like the Winter variety. Use it in chicken pot pies, herbed rice, and, for something quite different, in creamed onions.

SESAME SEED
Four thousand years ago, the Egyptians used sesame for its oil, grain and as a seasoning. We in the U.S. are indebted to the slaves who brought sesame from Africa as a reminder of their homeland.

This nut-like seed is sold untoasted, and may be used as an ingredient or a topping that will be baked or browned. But if you are going to use them as an ingredient, you must toast them first in a baking dish in a medium oven for 20 to 25 minutes. Stir until they are light brown and have a nutty flavor. You'll enjoy toasted sesame seeds on hamburgers, sprinkled over any salad, on green beans instead of almonds, and as sesame butter to serve with fresh water fish.

TARRAGON
Its sweet, aromatic anise-like taste and odor make one think of the tropics. But unlike most herbs and spices that are from the tropical and temperate zones, tarragon is from the steppes of Siberia. It is most popular in France where it is one of the four components of "Fines Herbes" (chervil, chives, parsley, and tarragon in equal amounts). Tarragon makes a wonderful wine vinegar. Use it to flavor mayonnaise, and in poultry and fish stuffings.

THYME

"You smell of thyme" was one of the finest compliments one ancient Greek could pay another. Thyme was the symbol of elegance. This herb came to America from France and Spain, and became one of our most prolific seasonings. It has a warm, fragrant aromatic odor and pungent taste, and is best used in making such diverse dishes as sauerbraten, chicken pot pie, pizza and spaghetti sauces, wine vinegars, and in salad dressings. Thyme butter is delightful over creamed white onions, braised celery, asparagus, green beans, eggplant and tomatoes.

TURMERIC

A stranger to most American kitchens, turmeric is a little-appreciated herb whose taste is somewhat peppery, but whose coloring attribute ranks it as the poor cousin of saffron. Like saffron it imbues a warm golden yellow color which is most appealing in making Spanish rice, curries, cheese spreads, and mustard sauces.

Appetizers
&
Light Foods

THE HERBS & SPICES COOKBOOK

29

Wild Mushroom Tarts

TART PASTRY:

2 cups flour
½ teaspoon salt
½ pound butter, chilled

2 egg yolks
4 tablespoons ice water

WILD MUSHROOM FILLING:

5 tablespoons butter
½ cup Champagne
5-6 shallots, minced
2 tablespoons Brandy
½ pound mushrooms, minced

1 ¾ cups heavy cream
4 eggs, beaten
¼ teaspoon cayenne pepper
Salt and white pepper

To prepare the pastry, combine the flour and salt in a food processor. Pulse briefly to sift. Add the butter, one tablespoon at a time, and process until crumbly. Now, add the egg yolks. Add the ice water and continue processing until dough just begins to form a ball. (Do not over process, or the dough will be tough.) Wrap in wax paper and refrigerate for 2 hours. Remove from the refrigerator and press into 4-inch tart pans.

The prepare the filling, melt 2 tablespoons of the butter in a small pan over medium heat. Add the Champagne. Sauté the shallots until all liquid is gone. Remove shallots and set aside.

In a medium pan over medium heat, melt the remaining 3 tablespoons of butter. Add the Brandy. Sauté the mushrooms until tender. Using a slotted spoon, remove the mushrooms and set aside. Reduce the liquid to ¼ cup; reserve.

In a medium bowl, whisk together the cream, eggs and cayenne pepper. Whisk in the reserved mushroom broth and season to taste with salt and white pepper.

Evenly spread the mushrooms and shallots in the tart shells. Pour in the cream mixture. Bake at 375 degrees for 20 to 30 minutes, or until set.   Makes 4 to 6 tarts.

Serve with Champagne or Sauvignon Blanc.

Herbed Quesadillas

These are one of our favorite party hors d'oeuvres since they are so easy and fast to make.

½ red onion, peeled and cut in ¾-inch slices
2 tablespoons vegetable oil
8 flour tortillas (8 inch)
1 red bell pepper, roasted, peeled and cut into ½-inch strips
½ pound low-fat mozzarella cheese, grated

2 garlic cloves, peeled and minced
2 tablespoons fresh marjoram (or 1 teaspoon dried)
2 tablespoons fresh oregano (or 1 teaspoon dried)
Pinch of freshly ground black pepper

Preheat a grill or broiler. Brush the onion slices with 1 tablespoon of the oil. Grill or broil 6 inches from the heat for 4 minutes on each side.

Heat a skillet over high heat. Soften the tortillas by grilling for 30 seconds on each side.

Mix the onion, red pepper strips, mozzarella, garlic, marjoram, oregano and pepper. Divide evenly over 4 tortillas and top with remaining 4, pressing them down gently. Brush both sides lightly with oil.

Preheat oven to 400 degrees. Bake the quesadillas for 3 to 5 minutes, or until lightly browned and the cheese is melted. Cut into quarters and serve immediately.   Makes 16 pieces.

Wine Note: One of the richer California Chardonnays or Sauvignon Blancs will balance the texture and flavors of this recipe.

Savory Stilton Cheese Tart

CRUST:

1 ¼ cups flour
¼ cup finely grated Parmesan
    cheese
¼ teaspoon salt

12 tablespoons butter (1 ½
    cubes)
1 egg yolk
3 tablespoons cold water

FILLING:

1 red onion, sliced
2 tablespoons butter
¼ cup Champagne
1 ½ cups heavy cream
6 egg yolks
¼ teaspoon salt

⅛ teaspoon cayenne pepper
⅛ teaspoon freshly grated
    nutmeg (optional)
¼ pound Stilton (or any blue
    cheese), crumbled

To prepare the crust, place the dry ingredients in a food processor. Pulse to blend. Add the butter and run the machine until the mixture is crumbly. Pour in the egg yolk and water. Run the machine until a ball of dough is formed. Cover and chill for 30 minutes or so.

For the filling, sauté the onion in the butter. Moisten with the Champagne, and simmer until the liquid is absorbed. Set aside. Whisk together the cream, eggs, salt, pepper and nutmeg.

Roll out the crust and press it into a 10-inch pan. Crumble the cheese inside and spread the onions on top. Pour the filling into the crust. Bake at 425 degrees for 10 minutes. Lower the temperature to 350 degrees and continue baking another 25 to 35 minutes, or until set. Serves 8.

Serve with Champagne, or a Cabernet Sauvignon.

Cilantro Salmon Tostada

1 cup dried small white beans
2 fresh jalapeño peppers
1 piece, 1-inch cube, salt pork
  (optional)
4 ounces fresh goat cheese
Corn oil
6 large or 12 small white corn
  tortillas
1 bunch cilantro

½ each red and yellow sweet
  peppers and red onion,
  chopped
A few drops of olive oil and
  rice wine vinegar
¼ pound smoked salmon,
  sliced thin
1 cup light sour cream

Soak the white beans according to package directions. Cut jalapeño peppers in half and remove seeds. Add the peppers along with the optional salt pork to the beans at the start of cooking. Cook according to package directions. When beans are tender, drain and remove pork and peppers, and let beans cool. Combine beans and goat cheese in food processor and purée.

Heat about 1 inch of corn oil in a heavy iron skillet and fry the tortillas just until they begin to color. Drain well on paper towels. Wash and de-stem cilantro. Combine sweet peppers and red onion, and moisten with a few drops of olive oil and rice wine vinegar.

To assemble, spread a little of the bean purée on each tortilla. Top with a handful of cilantro leaves and a slice of cured salmon. Spoon a little sour cream on, and sprinkle chopped peppers and onion over.   Serves 6.

Serve with Sauvignon Blanc.

Butternut Squash Pancake with
Baked Garlic Cream and Smoked Salmon

2-2 ½ cups coarsely grated
   butternut squash
1 medium onion, chopped
4 tablespoons unsalted butter
1 teaspoon chopped garlic
¼ teaspoon ground mace
¼ teaspoon marjoram
¼ teaspoon thyme
¼ teaspoon ground pepper
1 cup sifted all-purpose flour
1 tablespoon sugar

½ teaspoon baking powder
½ teaspoon salt
3 large eggs, lightly beaten
1 cup milk
15-20 thin slices of skinless
   butternut squash
2-3 heads of garlic
½ pint whipping cream
8-10 ounces sliced smoked
   salmon
2-3 whole chive spears

Sauté grated squash and onion in 1 tablespoon of the butter for 3 to 5 minutes until lightly browned. Add garlic, mace, marjoram, thyme and pepper, and sauté 1 to 2 minutes more. Remove from heat and cool to room temperature.

Combine flour, sugar, baking powder and salt. Make a well in the center of the mixture. Melt the remaining 3 tablespoons of the butter and mix with the eggs and milk into the well. Stir just until moistened (will be lumpy). Stir in squash-onion mixture gently. Spoon out approximately 2-ounce portions onto preheated lightly oiled griddle.

Sauté the squash slices in butter until they are golden brown. Season with sage, salt and pepper. Lay down 1 piece of sautéed squash on each pancake and barely cover with a bit more batter. Turn when lightly brown. Remove and let cool to room temperature.

To make the garlic cream, wrap the heads of garlic in foil, and bake in a 400 degree oven for 40 to 50 minutes until soft. Squeeze out garlic and mash. Whip heavy cream to soft peaks and add garlic purée, 1 to 2 teaspoons at a time, until nicely flavored. Season lightly with salt and pepper.

To serve, place a smoked salmon slice in rosette shape on top of pancake, fill center with garlic cream and garnish with 2 to 3 whole chive spears. Serves 8.

Serve with a Chardonnay.

Italian Gorgonzola Cheesecake

2 ounces Italian Gorgonzola
  cheese
2 tablespoons unsalted butter,
  softened
2 ounces cream cheese,
  softened
3 eggs

2 ½ tablespoons sour cream
1 ½ tablespoons minced fresh
  basil
⅛ teaspoon salt
¼ teaspoon white pepper
⅓ cup chopped walnuts

Heat oven to 350 degrees. Butter an 8-inch pie pan. In a food processor, cream Gorgonzola with butter until very smooth. Add the cream cheese and blend. Add the eggs one at a time, blending, until mixture is smooth. Add the sour cream, basil, salt and pepper, and mix well. Pour mixture into prepared pie pan and set the pie pan into a larger pan. Add enough hot water to come halfway up the side of the pie pan.

Bake in the oven until mixture is firm, golden and puffy, about 20 to 25 minutes. During the last 5 minutes of cooking, sprinkle top with the chopped walnuts. Finish baking. Remove from oven and allow to cool. Pie will collapse. Cut into slim wedges and serve with sliced baguette French bread.   Serves 6 to 8.

Serve with a Cabernet Sauvignon.

As another option, you may add caramelized red onions on top.

Zucchini Blossom Fritters with
Avocado Mousse and Smoked Tomato Sauce

8 baby zucchini with blossoms
1 small onion
¼ cup olive oil
1 tablespoon basil
Salt and pepper
½ avocado

4 ounces cream cheese
2 tablespoons lime juice
1 teaspoon chopped cilantro
Beignet Batter (recipe follows)
2 ounces Smoked Tomato
   Sauce (recipe follows)

Remove zucchini blossoms. Cut zucchini into ⅛-inch thin slices. Blanch and chill. Finely dice onion. Combine zucchini, onion, olive oil and basil, and season with salt and pepper. Mix avocado with cream cheese, add lime juice and cilantro. Stuff each blossom with 2 teaspoons of avocado/cream cheese mixture. Seal the top by pinching and twisting the open end gently. Prepare Beignet Batter.

BEIGNET BATTER:
½ cup flour
½ cup cornstarch
1 tablespoon oil (preferably
   nut oil)

1 egg
2 teaspoons baking powder
Water
Salt and pepper

Batter blossoms evenly in Beignet Batter and deep fry until golden brown. Drain well on paper towels. Prepare sauce.

SMOKED TOMATO SAUCE:
6 Roma tomatoes
½ yellow onion, chopped
2 teaspoons olive oil

2 garlic cloves, chopped
Salt and pepper

Smoke Roma tomatoes in smoker for approximately 6 minutes, then chop. Sweat onions in olive oil over low heat. Add tomatoes and garlic. Simmer for 30 minutes. Add salt and pepper. Purée and strain.

To serve, arrange zucchini-onion mixture around outside of plate; pour Smoked Tomato Sauce in center of plate. Place two fritters on sauce.   Serves 4.

Serve with a Fumé Blanc.

Potato-Parsnip Pancakes with Smoked Salmon, Lemon Sour Cream and Fresh Dill

2 large russet potatoes
2 medium parsnips
2 egg whites
¼ teaspoon ground nutmeg
Salt and freshly ground pepper
½ cup sweet unsalted butter,
   melted

12 ounces smoked salmon
½ cup sour cream
Zest of 1 lemon (chopped very
   fine) plus 2 tablespoons juice
4 large sprigs of fresh dill

TO PREPARE THE PANCAKES:
Preheat oven to 350 degrees. Peel potatoes and parsnips. Chop into small cube-size pieces that will fit in the feed tube of a food processor. Place the grating disk in your food processor and assemble the lid in place. Turn food processor on and put potato and parsnip cubes in feed tube. Press down through grating disk. To me, this is the easiest way to grate, but if you do not own a food processor, or you are not familiar with operating one, you may prefer to grate them with an old-fashioned grater.

Place grated potatoes and parsnips in a medium stainless steel bowl. In a separate bowl, beat the egg whites with a wire whisk. Add to the potatoes and parsnips. Add salt, pepper and nutmeg to potato-parsnip mixture. Combine well. Line a sheet pan with parchment paper. With a pastry brush, coat parchment paper with about ¼ of the melted butter.

Take a small amount of potato-parsnip mixture into the palm of your hand and mold into a pancake shape. Keep in mind that you will either want to divide the mixture into 4 sections for 1 large pancake per person, or 8 sections for 2 small pancakes per person. Once you have molded the pancake, place onto buttered sheet pan. Repeat process with remaining mixture. Brush the tops of the pancakes with ½ of the remaining butter.

Put pancakes into preheated oven. Bake for 20 to 25 minutes or until golden brown and crisp on the bottom. Remove pan from oven and flip pancakes over with metal spatula. Brush tops again with remaining melted butter. Bake again for 20 minutes or until golden brown. Remove from oven and keep in a warm place.

TO ASSEMBLE THE DISH:
Start by adding the lemon zest and juice to the sour cream. Stir thoroughly. Slice the smoked salmon into 1 ½-inch pieces. Place the pancakes in the center of each plate. Arrange the smoked salmon around the pancakes. Spoon the sour cream on top of each pancake and garnish with a sprig of dill.   Serves 4.

These pancakes are well worth the effort! They are baked slowly at a low temperature for the perfect texture from the potato and just the right sweetness from the parsnip. Once you try this recipe, you will love to make these pancakes for all occasions. They also go very well with homemade applesauce and sour cream.

Serve with a glass of Sparkling Wine.

Curried Chicken in Cracker Bread

4 chicken breasts, cooked and
  chopped
4 green onions, chopped
Fresh parsley, chopped
½-1 cup mayonnaise
Lemon juice
1 teaspoon curry

Salt and pepper
2 cracker breads
6 ounces cream cheese,
  softened with cream
1 small jar mango chutney
1 cup chopped peanuts
1 bag alfalfa sprouts

Combine chicken, green onions and parsley. Blend mayonnaise, lemon juice, curry, salt and pepper. Mix well with chicken.

To soften cracker bread, quickly wet cracker bread under running water (30 seconds) and place between cotton towels for ½ hour to absorb excess moisture.

Spread cracker bread evenly with softened cream cheese, chutney, chicken mixture and sprinkle with peanuts and sprouts. Roll up tightly and chill 4 hours. Slice into ¾-inch rolls.   Serves 8.

This dish is perfect for brunch, lunch or holiday parties. It is excellent accompanied by an off-dry, lightly fruity wine, such as a Gewürztraminer.

39

Four Cheeses Cheesecake

CARAMELIZED ONION/APPLE LAYER:
2 small onions   1 crisp apple
3 tablespoons butter   1 lemon, zested and juiced

NUT CRUST:
1 cup walnuts or pecans   ¼ cup cold butter
¼ cup flour   3 tablespoons cold water

CHEESE FILLING:
⅓ cup chopped fresh basil or   5 ounces Roquefort or
  oregano   Gorgonzola
8 ounces fresh ricotta cheese   ½ cup sour cream
8 ounces fresh goat cheese   1 whole egg
8 ounces fresh cream cheese

CARAMELIZED ONION/APPLE LAYER:
Peel onions and cut in half vertically. Lay flat and slice in thin, even slices. Over low heat, melt butter in a heavy saucepan, add onions and sauté slowly to caramelize for 30 to 45 minutes, turning frequently. Peel, core and shred the apple and toss with lemon juice. (Save lemon zest for cheese filling.) Set aside until onions are caramelized, then add to pan and sauté for several minutes. While onions are cooking, prepare crust and cheese filling.

NUT CRUST:
Lightly grease a 10-inch flat bottomed spring-form pan. Using a food processor, finely chop shelled nuts using the ON/OFF button. Put 2 tablespoons of the chopped nuts in the spring-form pan. Tilt and rotate to coat vertical sides of the pan, saving any loose nuts for garnish. Add flour and slices of cold butter to remaining nuts in processor, turning ON/OFF to blend. Add water and again blend quickly until nut-dough is formed. Press a thin layer on the bottom of the pan. Set aside.

CHEESE FILLING:
Wash, dry and de-stem basil. Finely chop in a food processor. Combine remaining ingredients, except the Roquefort, by using ON/OFF button to blend. Do not over process.

ASSEMBLY:

Preheat oven to 225 degrees. Spread caramelized onion/apple mixture on nut crust bottom. Crumble Roquefort on top of this mixture. Spoon cheese filling over top and spread evenly. Sprinkle remaining nuts on top. Fill a larger sided pan with 1 inch of hot water. Place the cheesecake in the center and bake in the water bath at 225 degrees for 2 hours or until set. This long, slow cooking insures a creamy texture. Remove from water bath and cool before sliding a clean knife around the edges to loosen. Remove side of spring-form pan. Allow to set up one hour before serving. Cut into wedge shaped pieces.   Serves 10 to 14.

Note: Take care to use dry, fresh onions and fresh, good quality cheeses that are not old, or the combined flavors will be too strong. This cheesecake can be covered with plastic wrap and refrigerated for several days. Use as an appetizer or light entrée to take the place of a cheese course, or for dessert.

Black Bean Salsa Dip

This is a great dip which is very highly seasoned.

2 cups drained black beans, cooked or canned
2 tablespoons olive oil
2 tablespoons fresh lime juice
1 ripe avocado, pitted, peeled and diced
½ cup canned corn kernels
1 green bell pepper, seeded and minced

1 red bell pepper, seeded and minced
½ cup minced red onion
2 jalapeño chilies, seeded and minced
½ teaspoon ground cumin
½ cup finely chopped fresh cilantro
Salt and black pepper

Combine beans, oil, lime juice and avocado in a food processor. Purée. Place blended mixture in a bowl, and add remaining ingredients. Mix well. Correct seasonings, if necessary, adding salt or lime juice to taste.   Makes 4 cups.

Serve with your favorite crackers.

Spicy Sesame Sticks

1 cup all-purpose flour
¼ teaspoon cayenne pepper
½ teaspoon dry mustard
½ teaspoon ground ginger
½ teaspoon salt
⅓ cup toasted sesame seeds*

½ cup grated sharp Cheddar
  cheese
1 egg, beaten
½ cup melted butter
½ to 1 tablespoon water

Heat oven to 350 degrees. Mix together the flour, pepper, mustard, ginger and salt. Stir in sesame seeds and cheese. Add the egg and melted butter. Stir and blend the ingredients, forming a ball. Add water, if needed. Cover dough and chill for 20 minutes.

Place dough on a floured surface and pat or roll to ¼-inch thickness. Cut in strips 1 inch wide and 3 or 4 inches long. Place on a flat cookie sheet.

Bake for 15 to 20 minutes, until lightly browned. Cool.

Makes 36 sticks.

*To toast sesame seeds, heat in a 350 degree oven for 20 minutes, stirring several times to toast evenly.

Spicy Herbed Nuts

2 tablespoons extra virgin olive
  oil
1 teaspoon dried thyme,
  crumbled
1 teaspoon salt

½ teaspoon cayenne
2 cups assorted nuts such as
  walnuts, pecans, hazelnuts,
  and almonds (with skins)

Preheat oven to 350 degrees.

In a bowl whisk together oil, thyme, salt, and cayenne. Add nuts and toss to coat well. Spread nuts in a shallow baking pan and roast in middle of oven 10 minutes. Nuts may be made 3 days ahead and kept in an airtight container.

Serve nuts warm.

Makes 2 cups.

Savory Focaccia

1 tablespoon yeast
2 cups all-purpose flour
2 tablespoons salt
3 tablespoons minced fresh
  basil
1 ½ tablespoons minced fresh
  rosemary

¼ cup olive oil
½ cup water
½ cup Chardonnay
¼ cup chopped crisp bacon
3 tablespoons minced onion,
  sautéed

Preheat oven to 450 degrees. Combine yeast, flour, salt, basil and rosemary. Add olive oil, water, Chardonnay, bacon and sautéed onion.

Knead to form dough. Let rise. Punch down and press into a 14-inch, well oiled pan. Allow to rise until dough has doubled. Bake 10 to 15 minutes until golden.

Serving suggestions: Top with smoked salmon, sour cream and chives. Or, use as a crust for a seafood pizza with your favorite shellfish and a mild cheese.

Serve with Chardonnay.

Green Olivado

1 10-ounce jar Spanish green
  olives
¼ cup blanched almonds
2 teaspoons fresh basil

1 teaspoon oregano
1 teaspoon thyme
¼ cup olive oil

Drain olives and rinse well. Soak in cold water 10 minutes, then drain thoroughly. Place olives, almonds and herbs in a food processor. Whirl to chop, and drizzle in olive oil while chopping. Serve with crackers or Middle Eastern pita bread.

                                   Makes 1 ½ cups.

Serve with Sauvignon Blanc or Fumé Blanc.

Cheddar-Herb Scones

2 cups unbleached flour	3 tablespoons chopped fresh
4 teaspoons baking powder	herbs (dill, basil, rosemary or
½ teaspoon baking soda	chives)
½ teaspoon salt	⅔ cup whipping cream
½ cup chilled, unsalted butter,	½ cup grated sharp Cheddar
cut in small pieces	cheese
1 egg	Additional cream

Preheat oven to 400 degrees. Stir together flour, baking powder, baking soda and salt. Cut in the butter pieces until mixture resembles coarse meal. In a separate bowl, whisk together the egg, herbs, whipping cream and cheese. Add to the dry ingredients and stir just to combine.

Turn dough onto a lightly floured board and knead about ten times. Roll out into a ½-inch thick rectangle and fold in half. Roll out a bit more to about ¾ inch thick. Cut out rounds with a floured cookie cutter. Brush tops of scones with additional cream and bake until golden, about 12 to 15 minutes. Makes approximately 12 scones.

Serve with Chardonnay.

Seared Venison Tartar with Pink Peppercorn Crust and Pickled Beets

8 ounces venison, ground through meat grinder on ¼-inch die
2 tablespoons diced sun-dried cherries
1 tablespoon vinegar
Salt and pepper
2-3 ounces of arugula

1 beet
½ cup rice wine vinegar
1 loaf olive bread, cut into slices
4 tablespoons pink peppercorns, crushed with rolling pin

Combine venison with sun-dried cherries, raspberry vinegar, and salt and pepper. Gently form into 4 patties. Press onto crushed peppercorns.

Clean the arugula. Boil the beet in rice wine vinegar until beet is tender. Peel and julienne the beet. Reserve with rice wine vinegar, and mix it with olive oil and salt to create a vinaigrette.

Brush olive bread with olive oil and bake in a 400 degree oven for 10 minutes.

Sear the venison patties in a sauté pan on the side with peppercorns only.

Arrange arugula in a circle on plates and place a venison patty in the middle. Garnish each plate with 2 olive bread slices and sprinkle with julienne beets. Drizzle with the vinaigrette.   Serves 4.

Wine Suggestion: Serve a Gamay Beaujolais.

Basil Pita Triangles with
Hummus and Red Pepper

5 whole wheat pita pockets   3 tablespoons olive oil
1 teaspoon basil, chopped   2 red bell peppers, roasted,
½ teaspoon Kosher salt   peeled and julienned

Preheat oven to 450 degrees. Cut each pita into 8 wedges. Toss wedges with basil, salt and oil. Place evenly on baking sheets and bake for 4 minutes on each side. Prepare Hummus.

HUMMUS:
1 can (15 ounces) chickpeas   1 clove garlic, minced
   with liquid   ½ teaspoon ground cumin
¼ cup lemon juice   ¼ cup cilantro (reserve some
½ cup Tahini (sesame paste)   leaves for garnish)
1 tablespoon olive oil   Salt and pepper

Combine all ingredients in food processor and process until smooth. Adjust seasoning.

Spread Hummus on pita triangles. Crisscross strips of red bell pepper over the top and garnish with a cilantro leaf.

Makes 40 pieces.

Sweet
Pepper

Blue Cheese Onion Pie

1 ½ cups cracker crumbs
6 tablespoons butter (at room temperature)
2 cups thinly sliced sweet onions (such as Vidalia, Walla Walla or Maui)
½ cup crumbled blue cheese
¾ cup cream
3 eggs
1 teaspoon salt
½ teaspoon black pepper
½ teaspoon marjoram
1 tablespoon finely minced parsley

Preheat oven to 350. Mix cracker crumbs and 4 tablespoons of the butter in a bowl until well blended. Press mixture on the bottom and sides of an 8-inch pie pan. Refrigerate.

Melt remaining 2 tablespoons butter in heavy skillet over medium heat. Sauté onions until soft and tender, about 10 minutes. Arrange onions on pie crust. Distribute the blue cheese over onions. Beat cream, eggs, salt, pepper and marjoram in medium bowl until blended. Pour egg mixture into crust over onions. Sprinkle with parsley. Bake pie for about 35 minutes, or until a knife inserted in center comes out clean. Slice and serve.   Makes 4 to 6 servings.

Serve with Chardonnay.

Smoked Salmon Puffs

1 cup minced fresh mushrooms
2 tablespoons butter
½ cup Chardonnay
½ cup heavy cream
½ cup plain cream cheese
1 cup chopped smoked salmon
Salt and pepper
2 tablespoons chopped fresh dill
24 small puff shells (can be purchased ready-made)

Sauté mushrooms in the butter until soft. Add wine and reduce by half. Add cream and reduce again by half. Cool; set aside. Combine the cheese and salmon with the wine-mushroom reduction. Mix thoroughly and season to taste with salt and pepper. Add dill, mix, and cool. Cut tops off puff shells. Fill with salmon cheese mixture. Place tops on shells and serve at room temperature.   Makes 24.

Serve with Chardonnay.

Soups

THE HERBS & SPICES COOKBOOK

Sherried Crab Soup

1 tablespoon butter
1 small onion, chopped
2 whole cloves
1 large bay leaf
1 tablespoon all-purpose flour
2 cups milk
1 cup whipping cream
⅛ teaspoon ground nutmeg

⅛ teaspoon cayenne pepper
½ pound fresh crabmeat, cleaned
1 bottle (8 ounces) clam juice
½ cup dry Sherry
Salt and pepper
¼ cup chopped fresh chives or small green onions

Melt butter in heavy large saucepan over medium heat. Add onion, cloves and bay leaf and sauté until onion is translucent, about 3 minutes. Sprinkle with flour and stir 1 minute. Gradually whisk in milk and cream. Add nutmeg and ⅛ teaspoon cayenne pepper. Reduce heat to medium-low. Simmer until slightly thickened, about 15 minutes.

Strain soup into bowl, removing cloves and bay leaf. Return liquid to same saucepan. Add crabmeat, clam juice and Sherry; simmer until thickened, about 15 minutes (do not boil). Season with additional cayenne pepper, if desired, and salt and pepper.

Ladle soup into bowls; garnish with chives.   Serves 4

Serve with Chardonnay or Sauvignon Blanc.

Tomato Soup Fumé

2 small onions, sliced
½ red bell pepper, seeded and
   chopped
2 stalks celery, chopped
½ cube butter
¼ cup flour
½ cup Fumé Blanc
1 tablespoon fresh dill, or 1
   teaspoon dry

½ teaspoon basil
½ teaspoon thyme
Salt and white pepper
6 cups canned ready-cut,
   peeled tomatoes (3 15-16
   ounce cans)
3 cups chicken stock
1 teaspoon sugar
½ bell pepper, chopped

Sauté onion, pepper and celery in the butter. Add the flour and sauté. Add the wine, dill, basil, thyme, salt and pepper to taste. Add tomatoes and stock, and simmer 15 minutes. Cool and purée in a blender or food processor.

Adjust seasonings and reheat soup. Serve in bowls topped with puff pastry* rounds that have been baked for 15 to 20 minutes until lightly browned.   Serves 6.

* *Ready-made puff pastry is available at specialty food stores or supermarkets in the cooler cabinets.*

Pumpkin Soup with Apples and Black Walnuts

1 large onion, chopped
4 garlic cloves, minced
1 stick unsalted butter
1 ½ pounds pumpkin, peeled, seeded and diced
4 Pippin apples (or other tart cooking apple), peeled, cored and sliced
1 cup chopped black walnuts
1 cup apple cider

5 cups chicken stock or canned broth
1 teaspoon crumbled sage
½ teaspoon chopped fresh thyme leaves
Salt and white pepper
1 cup heavy cream or half-and-half
½ cup finely chopped black walnuts

Sauté the onion and garlic in the butter over moderate heat, stirring until they are softened. Add the pumpkin, apples, chopped walnuts, cider, stock, sage, thyme, and salt and pepper to taste. Bring to a boil, reduce heat and simmer, partially covered, for about 45 minutes or until pumpkin is tender.

Purée the mixture in batches. Transfer to a pot and stir in the cream, being careful not to let it boil. Serve in bowls, and garnish with finely chopped walnuts. Serves 10.

Suggested wine: Chardonnay.

Ginger Pumpkin Soup

1 medium onion, minced
1 clove garlic, minced
2 tablespoons minced or finely grated ginger
2 tablespoons butter
2 cups chicken broth

2 cups cooked, mashed pumpkin
1 cup heavy cream
3 tablespoons dry Sherry
1 tablespoon lime juice

Sauté onion, garlic and ginger in butter until onion is transparent. Add chicken broth and pumpkin. Simmer for 20 minutes. Add cream, Sherry and lime juice. Reheat slowly. Serves 4.

Serve with a Gewürztraminer.

Curried Carrot Soup

1 large onion, chopped
1 teaspoon minced garlic
1 teaspoon minced ginger root
2 tablespoons unsalted butter
1 teaspoon curry powder
⅛ teaspoon cinnamon
3 ½ cups chicken stock
2 pounds carrots, peeled and
  chopped

1 bay leaf
⅛ teaspoon crumbled dried
  thyme
¼ teaspoon ground pepper
½ cup half-and-half
1 tablespoon honey
½ cup plain yogurt or heavy
  cream

In a kettle, cook onion, garlic and ginger in butter over moderate heat, stirring until onion is soft. Stir in curry powder and cinnamon and cook, stirring for 10 seconds. Add stock, carrots, bay leaf, thyme, pepper and ½ cup water. Bring to boil and simmer, covered, for 30 minutes.

Discard bay leaf. Let cool, then purée in 2 batches in blender until very smooth. Transfer to large saucepan and whisk in half-and-half, honey, and salt to taste; heat. Top each serving with a dollop of yogurt.   Makes 8 cups.

Salmon Bisque

4 tablespoons butter
½ cup minced white onion
½ cup finely chopped celery
2 tablespoons flour
½ teaspoon salt

½ teaspoon black pepper
3 cups milk
1 pound cooked salmon, flaked
1 cup cream
1 tablespoon minced fresh dill

Melt butter in a large pot. Cook onion and celery in the butter until tender. Blend in flour, salt and pepper. Add milk gradually. Cook until mixture thickens, stirring constantly.

Add salmon and simmer until hot. Add cream and stir. Serve with a garnish of fresh dill floated on top. Accompany with crispy crackers.
                                                                   Serves 6.

Cold Cucumber Soup with Dill

The perfect soup for a summer luncheon.

2 cups chicken stock
3 cucumbers, peeled, seeded
 and sliced
2 tablespoons chopped onion
1 tablespoon minced fresh dill
 (or 2 tablespoons dried)

Salt and freshly ground pepper
2 cups plain yogurt
½ cup finely chopped, toasted
 walnuts
Thin slices of unpeeled
 cucumber

In a 4-quart saucepan, combine stock, cucumbers and onion. Bring to a boil; reduce heat and simmer until cucumbers are just tender, about 5 to 7 minutes. Cool.

In a food processor, purée stock mixture, dill, salt and pepper to taste. Process until smooth (in batches if necessary). Add yogurt. Chill and adjust seasonings.

Before serving, stir in toasted walnuts. Serve cold, garnished with paper-thin slices of cucumber. Serve with crispy crackers.

Serves 4 to 6.

This delicate soup is best served with a Sauvignon Blanc.

Tortilla Soup

4 boneless chicken breasts
10 cups chicken stock
10 corn tortillas, torn in small
  pieces
4 ounces tomato purée
1 red onion, diced
3 cloves garlic, finely minced
1 large red bell pepper, diced

1 jalapeño pepper, seeded
  and finely diced
2 tablespoons olive oil
1 tablespoon cumin
1 tablespoon chili powder
1 tablespoon Worcestershire
  sauce

GARNISH:
2 small avocados, peeled and
  diced
½ cup shredded Cheddar
  cheese

¼ cup chopped fresh cilantro
Lime wedges
Tortilla chips

Poach chicken breasts in stock until done. Remove and put stock aside. Shred or dice chicken breasts; put aside. Add tortilla pieces to stock and simmer 10 minutes until soft. Purée stock in blender.

Add back to pot along with tomato purée and chicken. Sauté onions, garlic and peppers in oil. Add spices and Worcestershire sauce. Sauté until fragrant. Add to soup and simmer 15 minutes.

Divide soup into 8 bowls, sprinkle with avocados, cheese and cilantro. Serve with wedges of lime and tortilla chips.   Serves 8.

Recommended wine: A dry white wine.

Fresh Corn Chowder

3 strips lean bacon
2 tablespoons olive oil
1 large white onion, diced
2 stalks celery, diced small
2 carrots, peeled and diced
2 cloves garlic, minced
¾ cup Chardonnay
3 cups fresh corn kernels (cut from 6 ears of corn)

3 cups chicken stock
2 tablespoons chopped fresh thyme
2 tablespoons chopped fresh basil
1 cup cream
Salt and pepper to taste

In a soup pot, cook bacon until crisp. Remove bacon, crumble and set aside. Add the olive oil to the remaining bacon drippings and sauté the onion, celery, carrots and garlic until tender. Add the wine and simmer for several minutes over medium heat.

Add corn, chicken stock and thyme. Simmer until corn is tender. Put ⅓ of the mixture into a food processor and purée. Return to soup pot. Add basil, reserved bacon bits and cream. Reheat.

Season to taste with salt and pepper. Serve with crisp crackers.

Serves 6

Serve with a Chardonnay.

Cream of Carrot Soup with Dill

2 pounds roughly chopped
   carrots (about 5 ½ cups)
½ cup roughly chopped leek,
   white part only
2 ½ cups chicken stock,
   enough to barely cover the
   carrots and leeks
½ teaspoon salt
1 teaspoon Worcestershire
   sauce

2 tablespoons butter
2 tablespoons flour
3 cups milk
2 teaspoons chopped fresh dill
   weed
⅛ teaspoon white pepper
A few shakes of nutmeg
2 tablespoons dry Sherry

Put the carrots, leeks, stock, salt and Worcestershire in a sauce pot. Bring to a boil, then reduce heat and simmer for 20 minutes, or until the carrots are quite tender. Allow to cool, then purée in a food processor or blender. Make a roux of the butter and flour, stir in the milk and simmer for 10 minutes. Add the puréed carrots, dill, pepper and nutmeg. Heat slowly to prevent scorching. Add the Sherry just before serving.   Serves 6 to 8.

Red Bell Pepper Soup

2 pounds red bell peppers (10-12 medium peppers)	2 tablespoons olive oil
	4 cups chicken stock
1 onion, chopped	2 teaspoons coriander, minced
4 cloves garlic, chopped	6 tablespoons sour cream

Clean, de-seed and chop peppers. Sauté onions, garlic and peppers in olive oil until tender, approximately 10 minutes. Shake the pan occasionally to prevent burning. Add half of the chicken stock and cook for 10 more minutes.

At this point, either remove from heat to strain the mixture for a creamier texture, or leave as is for a chunkier soup.

Add the rest of the chicken stock. Simmer until the desired consistency is reached. Season with coriander. For a richer flavor, a little cream may be added. Remove from heat. Garnish each bowl with 1 tablespoon sour cream. Serve hot or cold.   Serves 6.

Try with Fumé Blanc or a Sauvignon Blanc.

Curried Chicken and Olive Soup

1 fryer chicken (2 to 3 pounds)
1 medium onion, quartered
2 stalks celery, cut in large
   pieces
2 carrots, cut in large pieces
2 large onions, sliced thin
2 large tart apples, sliced thin
3 tablespoons olive oil
½ teaspoon salt
½ teaspoon black pepper

1 teaspoon chili powder
1 teaspoon curry powder
4 tablespoons flour
1 cup Sauvignon Blanc
2 cups frozen peas
1 cup milk
⅔ cup sliced stuffed green
   olives
1 cup cream

Boil the chicken in 4 cups water with the quartered onion, celery and carrot pieces for approximately 1 hour, until chicken is tender. Remove chicken and cool. Strain broth and reserve 3 cups. Dice 2 cups of the chicken.

Fry the sliced onions and apples in olive oil, adding the salt, pepper, chili powder, curry powder and flour. Mix well. Add the wine, reserved 3 cups of chicken broth and the peas. Cook until tender, stirring frequently.

Add the milk, diced chicken and sliced olives. Bring to a boil. Add cream and serve hot.   Serves 6

Serve with Sauvignon Blanc.

Brandied Peach and Plum Soup

The soup may be served cold or hot. Try it first hot, then again after it has been chilled before deciding on your preference.

2 cups peeled and sliced ripe peaches
2 cups peeled and sliced ripe plums
1 ½ cups water
1 ½ cups dry white wine

⅔ cup sugar
1 lemon slice
1 cinnamon stick
3 tablespoons Brandy
Mint leaves for garnish

Place the peaches, plums, water, wine, sugar, lemon slice and cinnamon in a medium saucepan. Bring to a boil, lower heat and simmer gently for about 20 minutes or until fruit is fork-tender.

Allow mixture to cool before pressing through a chinois or sieve. Discard coarse pulp. Set soup aside to cool. Add Brandy and adjust to taste, adding sugar and/or Brandy as needed. Chill for 3 hours or longer.

Serve in chilled cups and garnish with finely chopped mint leaves.
Serves 4 to 5.

African Squash Soup

2 cups cooked pumpkin (canned)
3 tablespoons peanut butter
¼ teaspoon ground nutmeg
¼ teaspoon ground ginger
⅛ teaspoon lemon pepper

⅛ teaspoon salt
2 cups chicken broth
1 cup light cream
2 tablespoons chopped fresh parsley

Put pumpkin, peanut butter, nutmeg, ginger, pepper, salt and 1 cup of the chicken broth in a blender. Blend well to a smooth purée. Pour into a large saucepan and add balance of broth; mix.

Stir over medium heat until it just comes to a boil. Reduce heat and add cream. Warm again. Serve sprinkled with fresh chopped parsley.
Serves 4 to 6.

Tomato Provencal Soup

These flavors are typical of both Provence and California. The orange zest and licorice flavors (fennel, anise, tarragon) add a delicious accent.

8 tomatoes, or 4 cups canned, ready-cut peeled tomatoes
1 leek, diced
1 onion, chopped
4 cloves garlic, minced
½ fresh fennel bulb, chopped
2-3 tablespoons olive oil
3 cups chicken stock
¼ cup uncooked rice
1 bay leaf
1 tablespoon chopped fresh basil (or 1 teaspoon dry)

2 teaspoons fresh thyme (or ½ teaspoon dry)
1 tablespoon fennel or anise seed
Pinch saffron
Salt and fresh cracked pepper
4 tablespoons tomato paste
1 carrot, peeled and shredded or julienned
1 teaspoon fresh orange zest
4-6 tablespoons minced fresh parsley

Peel fresh tomatoes, cut in half and squeeze out the seeds and juice into a sieve set over a bowl. Reserve juice. (If using canned tomatoes, drain tomatoes, and reserve liquid.) Dice tomato pulp. Sauté the leek, onion, garlic and fennel in the olive oil until tender, approximately 2 to 3 minutes.

Mix tomato pulp with the sautéed vegetables and stir over low heat for about 1 minute. Add juice from tomatoes and the chicken broth and bring to a boil. Then add rice, bay leaf, basil, thyme, fennel and saffron. Simmer for 30 minutes. Stir in tomato paste, shredded carrot and orange zest, and remove from heat. Season to taste with salt and pepper. When ready to serve, garnish with fresh parsley.

Serves 6.

Delicious with Grenache Rosé.

Variation: Add ½ to 1 cup of shellfish (scallops, clams, shrimp, or crab) 5 to 7 minutes before serving.

Eggplant Soup

1 medium eggplant (1 pound)
2 medium yellow onions,
  peeled and thinly sliced
⅓ cup minced shallots or
  scallions
2 cups cored, seeded and
  chopped red bell peppers
6 cloves garlic, minced
⅓ cup olive oil
½ teaspoon dried basil
½ teaspoon dried thyme

½ teaspoon dried oregano
¼ teaspoon red pepper flakes
3 cups diced tomatoes
  (canned or fresh)
2 quarts chicken or vegetable
  stock
1 cup Fumé Blanc
Crème fraîche or sour cream
Freshly chopped chives (for
  garnish)

Slice unpeeled eggplant into rounds and place in one layer on a lightly oiled baking sheet. Sauté onions, shallots, red bell pepper and garlic in olive oil until soft, but not brown. Spread evenly over the top of the eggplant rounds and roast in preheated 425 degree oven for 15 to 20 minutes or until the eggplant is soft and lightly browned. Be careful that the topping doesn't burn.

In a food processor or blender, purée the eggplant along with the herbs, tomatoes, and stock. Place in a large soup pot with the wine, and gently reheat just to a boil. Correct seasoning and thin with additional stock if needed. Divide into bowls and garnish with a dollop of crème fraîche or sour cream and freshly chopped chives.

Serves 10 to 12.

Recommended wine: Fumé Blanc.

Black Bean Chili

1 ½ pounds dried black beans
3 tablespoons olive oil
2 large or 3 medium onions,
  chopped
6 large garlic cloves, minced
1 bay leaf
4 teaspoons ground cumin
2 tablespoons sweet
  Hungarian paprika
½ teaspoon cayenne pepper
1 green bell pepper, seeded
  and diced
4 tablespoons chili powder
3 tablespoons dried oregano
6-8 sun-dried tomatoes,
  chopped, to make ⅓ cup
1 can (28 ounces) tomatoes,
  seeded and chopped, with
  juice
½ teaspoon salt
½ teaspoon sugar
¼ cup mild taco sauce
1 tablespoon cider vinegar
Freshly ground black pepper
¼ cup chopped fresh cilantro,
  plus sprigs for garnish
6 tablespoons plain yogurt
6 tablespoons salsa

Soak beans overnight; drain. Heat 1 tablespoon of the olive oil over medium heat in a large stockpot. Sauté 1 cup of the onions with 2 teaspoons of the garlic for 5 minutes, or until the onions begin to soften. Add beans, about 8 cups water, or enough to cover the beans by an inch, and bay leaf. Bring to a boil. Reduce heat to low, cover and simmer for 1 to 2 hours.

Meanwhile, in a small dry skillet, heat cumin over medium heat, stirring until it just begins to smell fragrant. Remove from heat and add paprika and cayenne. Stir together in hot pan for less than a minute. Add chili powder and oregano. Stir and put aside.

In a second large casserole dish or stockpot, heat the remaining 2 teaspoons oil and sauté the remaining 1 cup onions over medium-low heat until they soften, about 5 minutes. Add 2 teaspoons of the remaining garlic and the green pepper, and continue to cook for about 5 minutes. Add spices and sun-dried tomatoes, stirring constantly, for about 3 to 5 minutes, scraping the bottom of the pan carefully so that the spices don't burn. If they cake or stick on the bottom of the pan, add a little water.

Add tomatoes and their juice, salt and sugar and bring to a simmer. Cover and simmer over low heat for 30 minutes, stirring often.

Add the beans with their liquid to the tomato mixture. Add the remaining 2 teaspoons garlic and taco sauce. Stir together and continue simmering, covered, for 2 hours or until the beans are thoroughly tender and the broth is thick and fragrant. For a thicker chili, simmer uncovered for the last half-hour of cooking. Remove bay leaf, stir in vinegar and pepper and adjust the seasonings. Stir in the cilantro just before serving.

To serve, ladle a generous portion of chili into each of six bowls and top with 1 tablespoon each of yogurt and salsa. Garnish with a few leaves of cilantro.
Serves 6.

Serve with Petite Sirah or Zinfandel.

Jamaican Red Bean Soup

1 pound boneless smoked
  ham, cut into ½-inch cubes
4 cups canned red kidney
  beans, drained and rinsed
3 ½ cups beef broth
2 cups cubed white potatoes
  (½-inch cubes)
2 cups cubed sweet potatoes
  (½-inch cubes)
¾ cup chopped celery

1 cup chopped onion
1 ½ teaspoons crushed thyme
½ teaspoon ground allspice
¼ teaspoon ground red
  pepper
¼ teaspoon ground black
  pepper
1 cup sweet Vermouth
2 tablespoons cornstarch

In a large saucepan, combine ham with 2 ½ cups water, beans, broth, potatoes, sweet potatoes, celery, onion, thyme, allspice and red and black peppers. Bring to a boil. Reduce heat and simmer, covered, until potatoes are tender, about 25 minutes.

Add Vermouth. Combine cornstarch with ½ cup cold water in a small bowl. Mix until smooth. Stir into soup and bring to a boil. Stir until slightly thickened, about 1 minute.
Serves 6.

Serve with a Merlot.

Salads

THE HERBS & SPICES COOKBOOK

Shrimp & Citrus Salad with Curry Dressing

2 cups torn butter lettuce, cleaned and in bite-size pieces
2 cups torn romaine leaves, cleaned and in bite-size pieces

1 medium red onion peeled and thinly sliced
2 navel oranges peeled and sectioned
1 pound small fresh cooked shrimp

CURRY MUSTARD DRESSING:
¼ cup red wine vinegar
2 teaspoons fresh lemon juice
2 teaspoons soy sauce
1 teaspoon sugar
1 teaspoon Dijon mustard

½ teaspoon curry powder
½ teaspoon salt
¼ teaspoon ground pepper
⅔ cup olive oil

To prepare the dressing, blend vinegar, lemon juice, soy sauce, sugar, mustard, curry powder, salt and pepper in processor until well blended. Gradually add olive oil and blend well. Makes 1 cup.

Combine lettuce and arrange on individual salad plates. Divide and arrange onion slices and orange pieces among plates. Spoon 2 tablespoons of curry mustard dressing over each salad. Top with shrimp. Serve immediately. Serves 4 to 6.

Serve with hot rolls and a Sauvignon Blanc.

Oven-Dried Tomato Salad with Herb Dressing

6 large ripe Roma tomatoes, cut   ¼ cup olive oil
   in half   6 cups mixed salad greens

Rub each tomato half with olive oil and place on a baking sheet.
Season each with salt and pepper. Place in a 200 degree oven for
5 to 6 hours, until they are half dried. Chill.

HERB DRESSING:
½ cup white wine   1 teaspoon fresh thyme
½ cup olive oil   2 tablespoons fresh parsley
1 tablespoon fresh basil   2 cloves garlic, peeled
1 tablespoon fresh oregano

Purée all the ingredients in a blender.

To serve, divide salad greens on 6 plates, place tomatoes on salad
greens, ladle a small amount of the dressing on each oven-dried
tomato. Garnish with a grind of fresh black pepper.   Serves 6.

Serve with a Chardonnay.

Pasta Salad with Sesame Dressing

1 package (12 ounces) rotelle pasta
2 cloves garlic, minced
1 2-inch piece fresh ginger, peeled and minced
3 tablespoons soy sauce
2 tablespoons wine vinegar
¼ cup olive oil
2 tablespoons sesame oil

1 teaspoon Tabasco sauce (hot pepper sauce)
2 tablespoons sesame seeds
1 large bell pepper, cleaned and chopped
2 cups thinly sliced green onions including part of green

Cook rotelle according to package instructions. Drain. Rinse with cool water. Drain again and put aside to cool.

To make the dressing, place garlic and ginger in food processor. Process until very fine. Add soy sauce and vinegar, blend. Combine olive and sesame oils and gradually add to contents. Add hot pepper sauce. Process until well blended.

Heat sesame seeds in a skillet over medium heat stirring for 1 to 2 minutes. Remove from heat.

Combine rotelle, dressing, bell pepper and onions. Toss sesame seeds through salad and serve.   Serves 6.

Serve with Zinfandel.

Chicken Waldorf Salad

2 cups cubed cooked chicken
  breast (2 half breasts)
½ cup diced celery
2 Red Delicious apples, cut
  into small cubes
2 tablespoons chopped
  walnuts

1 cup green seedless grapes
2 tablespoons mayonnaise
1 tablespoon nonfat yogurt
¼ teaspoon ground nutmeg
¼ teaspoon ground cinnamon
4 cups mixed salad greens

In a medium bowl, combine chicken, celery, apples, walnuts and grapes. In a small bowl, combine mayonnaise, yogurt, nutmeg and cinnamon; mix well. Pour over chicken mixture and toss. Cover and refrigerate for 1 hour to blend flavors before serving.

To serve, arrange salad greens on 4 plates. Spoon ¾ cup of the chicken mixture over each.　　　　　　　　　　　Makes 4 servings.

Serve with warm dinner rolls and a chilled Johannisberg Riesling.

Spicy Black Bean Salad

5 cups cooked black beans
1 red onion, minced
2 large tomatoes, seeded and
  chopped
½ cup chopped fresh cilantro
3 jalapeño peppers, seeded
  and minced
3 cloves garlic, minced

2 tablespoons lemon or lime
  juice
1 ½ teaspoons ground cumin
2 tablespoons red wine
  vinegar
½ cup olive oil
1 teaspoon salt
¼ teaspoon ground pepper

Rinse the black beans under cold, running water. Drain thoroughly.

In a large mixing bowl, combine beans with onion, tomatoes, cilantro, peppers, garlic, lemon juice, cumin, vinegar, oil, salt and pepper. Toss gently until mixed. This salad can be covered and refrigerated for up to 2 days.　　　　　　　　　　Serves 10 to 12.

Serve with Cabernet Franc.

Thai Chicken Salad

A very traditional Thai salad with a refreshing minty ginger flavor.

4 chicken breasts, cooked and cut into ¾ inch cubes
1 cucumber, peeled, seeded and chopped
2 cups fresh bean sprouts
2 fresh green chiles, seeded and chopped fine
½ red onion, sliced thin and broken into rings
1 tablespoon fresh grated ginger
½ cup fresh chopped cilantro (stems and leaves)
Lime-Mint Dressing (see recipe below)
¼ cup chopped roasted peanuts

In a large bowl, combine chicken and cucumber. In another bowl, combine bean sprouts, chiles, onion, and ginger. If not serving immediately, cover and refrigerate ingredients. Prepare dressing.

LIME-MINT DRESSING:
¼ cup lime juice
3 tablespoons soy sauce
2 tablespoons vegetable oil
5 teaspoons sugar
1 tablespoon chopped fresh mint leaves
2 cloves minced garlic
¼ teaspoon salt

Stir dressing ingredients until sugar dissolves.

At serving time, combine chicken-cucumber mixture, bean sprout mixture, cilantro, and Lime-Mint Dressing. Sprinkle with chopped peanuts and serve with toasted pita bread cut in wedges.

Makes 4 to 6 servings.

A Gewürztraminer wine will complement the interesting flavors in this salad.

Mixed Lettuce Greens
with Basil Oil and Blue Cheese

2 bunches basil
1 cup olive oil
1 head radicchio
1 head Belgian endive
2 bunches watercress or
   arugula
2 heads butter lettuce

1 tablespoon Champagne or
   white wine vinegar
Juice of ½ of a lemon
1 teaspoon salt
2-3 ounces blue cheese,
   crumbled

Remove leaves from one of the bunches of basil and reserve. Add stems to the second bunch of basil and blanch in 2 quarts boiling water for 15 seconds. Quickly refresh under cold running water, pat dry and coarsely chop. Measure the basil and place equal parts of basil and olive oil in a blender and make a smooth paste. Remove and add 3 parts oil to 1 part purée. Shake to combine thoroughly and let settle 24 hours. Strain basil oil through a paper coffee filter. Store strained oil tightly covered in the refrigerator for up to 1 week.

Rinse and thoroughly dry all salad greens. Keep small leaves whole; tear large leaves into pieces. Add reserved basil leaves.

Make a vinaigrette with ½ cup of the basil oil, Champagne vinegar, lemon juice and salt. Toss the lettuces and basil in vinaigrette and top with crumbled blue cheese.   Serves 4.

Wine suggestion: Cabernet Sauvignon.

Artichokes Stuffed with Smoldering Shrimp

12 medium artichokes
Juice of 1 lemon (retain rind)
3 tablespoons butter
1 cup finely minced white
  onion
⅓ cup chopped celery
6 cloves garlic
1 tablespoon thyme leaves

½ teaspoon oregano leaves
½ teaspoon cayenne pepper
1 ½ pounds cream cheese
¼ cup mayonnaise
2 red bell peppers, peeled by
  roasting
2 pounds cooked bay shrimp
Chopped parsley for garnish

Prepare artichokes for cooking by removing tough outer leaves until you reach lighter, inner leaves. Trim off tops and stems. Cut out the inedible prickly choke from the heart of the artichoke and discard (trimming away all hard, inedible part).

Boil artichokes in water with lemon juice and rind until done. Drain upside down overnight in a covered pan in the refrigerator.

In sauce pan, melt butter, then sauté onions and celery until slightly translucent. Add garlic, then thyme, oregano and cayenne. Cook several minutes, stirring, then remove from heat.

Blend cream cheese, mayonnaise and bell peppers in food processor. When finished, transfer to a bowl. Then add the shrimp. Mix well and refrigerate.

Stuff artichokes and serve. Top with a garnish of finely chopped parsley.   Serves 12.

Serve with Chardonnay.

75

Grilled Scallop Salad with Basil Vinaigrette Dressing

½ cup olive oil
1 teaspoon Dijon mustard
1 garlic clove, minced
1 bunch of freshly chopped
  parsley
Salt and pepper
12 sea scallops

2 bell peppers, preferably red
  and yellow
1 bunch arugula
A mixture of mâche and red
  oak leaf lettuce
Basil Vinaigrette (recipe
  follows)

Combine oil, mustard, garlic, parsley, and salt and pepper to taste. Add scallops and let stand for one hour at room temperature. Place two scallops on each skewer.

Roast peppers, peel, seed and slice into julienne strips. Reserve separately. Clean lettuce greens. Combine and reserve. Grill scallops for about 1 ½ to 2 minutes.

BASIL VINAIGRETTE:
¼ cup balsamic vinegar
¼ cup Sherry vinegar
½ orange, juiced
2 shallots
1-2 bunches basil, depending
  upon desired flavor

1 ½ cups extra virgin olive
  oil
Salt and pepper
1 anchovy fillet, optional

Prepare vinaigrette by combining all ingredients except oil In a blender or food processor. Blend until mixture becomes a smooth paste. With machine running, gradually add olive oil. Add salt and pepper to taste. Set aside.

Toss salad greens very lightly with Basil Vinaigrette and divide onto serving plates. Top each plate with sliced scallops and julienned roasted peppers, and drizzle remaining dressing on top. Serve immediately.   Serves 6.

Serve with Chardonnay.

Orange Pecan Chicken Salad

8 cups torn leaves of butter lettuce

4 cooked skinless chicken breasts, cooled and cut into long strips

2 teaspoons minced fresh marjoram leaves (or 1 teaspoon crumbled dry marjoram)

2 teaspoons grated fresh orange peel

¼ teaspoon crushed dry hot red pepper

Lemon Dressing (recipe follows)

Salt

½ cup freshly-toasted pecans, cut into lengthwise slivers

Toss the lettuce, chicken, marjoram, orange peel and red pepper with enough dressing to coat generously, and salt to taste. Arrange on four dinner plates. Sprinkle with nuts. Accompany with crusty French rolls. Makes 4 main course servings.

LEMON DRESSING:

2 tablespoons fresh lemon juice

1 teaspoon sugar

½ teaspoon salt

1 teaspoon minced green onions (white part only)

½ cup light olive oil

Combine lemon juice, sugar, salt and green onions. Gradually whisk in olive oil.

Serve with a white wine.

Baked Chèvre Salad with Fuji Apples and Toasted Pecans

This is a great combination of flavors and is a really simple salad to prepare for either a first course or as an entrée salad.

¼ cup plus 3 tablespoons
   butter
1 cup pecans, freshly toasted
½ cup sugar
10 ounces chèvre cheese
½ cup safflower oil
2 cups fresh bread crumbs
2 fuji apples

8 cups mixed greens
2 tablespoons blackberry
   vinegar
3 tablespoons sparkling wine
3 tablespoons finely chopped
   fresh thyme
Salt and freshly ground pepper

TO BREAD THE CHÈVRE:
Portion the chèvre into 4 equal pieces. Mold each piece into a thick patty shape. Dip each patty into the oil, then dip into the bread crumbs. You will want to cover the entire piece of cheese with bread crumbs, so be sure and pack the bread crumbs firmly with the palm of your hand. Transfer the breaded chèvre onto a sheet pan lined with parchment or foil. Preheat oven to 350 degrees. Place the chèvre in preheated oven. Chèvre should be baked for 10 minutes.

TO PREPARE SALAD:
While the chèvre is in the oven, you can prepare the rest of the salad. Cut the fuji apples into ¼-inch slices and set aside. Melt the ¼ cup butter in a medium sauté pan on low heat. Once the butter is completely melted, add the apples and cook for about 4 minutes. The apple slices should appear to have little extra color, but you do not want them to be too soft. Then, put them in a stainless steel bowl. Add the mixed greens, blackberry vinegar, sparkling wine and fresh thyme.

Toss salad with tongs until it is well incorporated. Season to taste with salt and pepper.

Remove chèvre from oven when it has been in the oven for the full 10 minutes. Portion the greens mixture onto 4 plates and place the baked chèvre on top of the salad. Place about 6 toasted pecans around each salad. You can add more if you like.   Serves 4.

Sit back and enjoy this wonderful salad with a glass of sparkling wine.

Chicken Bulgur Salad

¾ cup bulgur wheat
¾ cup boiling water
2 cups cubed cooked chicken
2 medium tomatoes, peeled,
   seeded and chopped
¼ cup chopped basil
2 tablespoons olive oil
2 tablespoons red wine
   vinegar

1 garlic clove, minced
1 tablespoon chopped mint
   leaves
Salt and pepper to taste
1 head romaine lettuce,
   separated into leaves
½ cup minced parsley for
   garnish

Combine bulgur and boiling water in a small bowl. Cover and set aside for about 20 minutes until bulgur has absorbed water and is soft and fluffy.

In a salad bowl, toss bulgur with chicken, tomatoes, basil, oil, vinegar, garlic, and mint; season with salt and pepper to taste.

To serve, mound salad on a bed of romaine lettuce; garnish with parsley.   Makes 4 to 6 servings.

Serve with a Chardonnay.

Baby Lettuce Salad with Prawns and Grapefruit

16 medium prawns, peeled
 and deveined
1 cup Sauvignon Blanc
1 teaspoon chopped fresh (or
 ½ teaspoon dried) tarragon
16 pink grapefruit sections

1 cup light olive oil
Salt and pepper
4 cups mixed baby lettuces,
 washed thoroughly and dried
1 teaspoon minced fresh
 chives

Poach prawns in the wine with half of the tarragon, until prawns turn just barely pink. Remove from heat and let cool in the liquid while preparing the grapefruit sections.

Drain prawns, reserving the liquid. Strain liquid into a small saucepan and reduce over medium heat until liquid is about ¼ cup. Let cool, then whisk in olive oil until thickened. Add the remaining tarragon, salt and pepper as needed.

Place lettuce on 4 chilled salad plates. Arrange prawns and grapefruit in alternating circle on each plate. Drizzle with dressing and sprinkle with the chives.   Serves 4.

Serve with Sauvignon Blanc.

Warm Mushroom Salad with Champagne Vinaigrette and Goat Cheese Croutons

16 slices (¾ inch thick)
  sourdough or French
  baguette
6 tablespoons butter, melted
8 tablespoons soft goat
  cheese
2 small heads red or green
  leaf lettuce, washed

1 cup extra virgin olive oil
½ cup Champagne
Grated zest of 2 lemons
½ teaspoon freshly ground
  black pepper
2 teaspoons salt
½ pound mushrooms, sliced

Preheat oven to 400 degrees.

To make the croutons, brush the bread with butter and toast in oven. Spread with the cheese, and set aside.

Tear the lettuce into bite-size pieces and place in a mixing bowl.

In a small saucepan over medium heat, whisk together the olive oil, Champagne, lemon zest, black pepper and salt. Heat until simmering, then add the mushrooms.

Pour the warm mushroom dressing over the lettuce and toss. Serve immediately with the croutons. Serves 8.

Serve with Champagne.

Mediterranean Pasta Salad

1 pound fusilli or corkscrew
   pasta
½ cup plus 3 tablespoons
   extra virgin olive oil
3 tablespoons Brut
   Champagne
6 cups plum tomatoes,
   quartered
½ cup sliced black olives
½ cup sliced green olives
½ cup chopped basil

1 cup finely sliced scallions
¼ cup capers
4 slices lean bacon, cooked
   and crumbled
2 tablespoons balsamic
   vinegar
1 teaspoon ground turmeric
2 teaspoons ground cumin
Salt and freshly ground black
   pepper

Cook the pasta in boiling, salted water according to package directions until tender. Drain and rinse in cold water to stop the cooking process. Toss with 3 tablespoons of the olive oil and the Champagne.

Combine the tomatoes, olives, basil, scallions, capers and bacon. Toss to coat with the ½ cup olive oil, vinegar, turmeric, cumin and salt and pepper to taste. Add this mixture to the pasta.

Refrigerate if serving in more than an hour. Otherwise, serve this salad at room temperature as an accompaniment to grilled fish or chicken.   Serves 10.

Serve with Brut Champagne.

Raspberry Rose Salad

6 large handfuls of red leaf
   lettuces -- oak leaf, lolla
   rosa, radicchio, etc.
3 edible pink or rose-colored
   roses (raised without
   herbicides or pesticides)

5 tablespoons olive oil
1 ½ tablespoons raspberry
   vinegar
Salt and pepper
1 cup fresh raspberries

Wash and dry the lettuces, and tear into bite-size pieces (if necessary). Remove petals from roses and put aside.

Toss greens with the oil until well coated, then sprinkle on vinegar, salt, pepper, and raspberries and toss again.

Divide among six salad plates and scatter rose petals over each.

Serves 6.

Serve with Rosé wine.

Fusilli Pasta with Shrimp Salad

1 pound fusilli pasta
1 pound cooked bay shrimp
½ cup mayonnaise
¼ cup white wine
Juice of 1-2 lemons
1 green bell pepper, finely
   chopped

1 red bell pepper, finely
   chopped
1 cup celery, finely chopped
3 green onions, minced
Zest of 1 lemon
1 tablespoon minced tarragon
1 tablespoon minced parsley

Cook the pasta according to package directions until tender; drain and rinse. Combine the shrimp, mayonnaise, wine, lemon juice, peppers, celery, onions, lemon zest and herbs. Blend thoroughly with the cooked spaghetti. Chill several hours before serving.

Serves 4.

Serve with Sauvignon Blanc.

Easy Three Bean Salad

2 cups kidney beans (canned)
2 cups pinto beans (canned)
2 cups garbanzo beans
  (canned)
2 cups canned corn
½ cup sliced green onions

1 cup finely diced celery
¼ cup chopped parsley
2 jalapeño chile peppers,
  seeded and minced
Dressing (recipe follows)

Drain liquid from all cans, rinse the beans and corn, and drain. Mix beans, corn, onions, celery, parsley and jalapeños. Prepare dressing.

DRESSING:
¾ cup oil
½ cup vinegar
1 large garlic clove, chopped
1 ½ teaspoons salt

1 teaspoon chili powder
1 teaspoon oregano
¼ teaspoon ground cumin
⅛ teaspoon Tabasco

Combine dressing ingredients, mixing well. Add dressing to the bean salad and toss. Chill 6 hours or overnight.   Serves 10 to 12.

Serve with a Gewürztraminer.

Curried Chicken Salad

4 cups cubed cooked chicken
  breasts
1 cup cubed apple
1 cup chopped walnuts
1 cup seedless grapes

1 cup pineapple tidbits
½ cup mayonnaise
1 teaspoon curry powder
2 tablespoons lemon juice

Put chicken, fruit and walnuts into a large bowl; mix carefully. In a small bowl, mix the mayonnaise, curry powder and lemon juice thoroughly. Add to the chicken. Refrigerate for at least 1 hour.

Serves 6 to 8.

Red Potato Salad

1 pound small red potatoes, quartered
3 tablespoons crumbled blue cheese
4 tablespoons plain yogurt
2 tablespoons fresh lemon juice
¼ cup chopped fresh basil
Salt and black pepper
White wine, if needed
2 tablespoons thinly sliced green onions
1 tablespoon chopped fresh parsley

Bring water to a boil in a large pot. Add potatoes and boil for 15 to 20 minutes.

While potatoes are cooking, prepare the dressing by blending the blue cheese into the yogurt. Add lemon juice and basil. Season to taste with salt and pepper. If dressing is too thick, add wine to thin.

Pour dressing over potatoes and toss. Add green onions and parsley, tossing well. Serve at room temperature.   Serves 4.

Chicken Cantaloupe Salad with Ginger Dressing

2 cups cubed cooked chicken
1 cup sliced celery
1 cup green seedless grapes, halved
½ cup sliced almonds
1 cantaloupe, seeded, peeled and cubed

DRESSING:
½ cup mayonnaise
¼ cup sour cream
1 tablespoon fresh lemon juice
1 ½ teaspoons grated lemon peel
1 ½ teaspoons sugar
½ teaspoon powdered ginger

In a large bowl, combine salad ingredients. In a small bowl, combine dressing ingredients. Pour dressing over salad mixture and toss gently.
                                                              Serves 6.

Pastas
&
Grains

THE HERBS & SPICES COOKBOOK

Fettuccini in Basil Cream

3 tablespoons olive oil
3 tablespoons butter
1-2 cloves garlic, minced
3-4 tomatoes, peeled, seeded
  and chopped
½ cup dry white wine
½ cup heavy cream

½ cup finely chopped fresh
  basil leaves
Salt and white pepper
1 pound fettuccine (fresh is
  best)
Freshly grated Parmesan
  cheese

Heat oil and butter in a heavy saucepan over medium heat. Gently sauté garlic for a minute, then add tomatoes. Simmer until they soften, then add wine and cream. Simmer 5 to 10 minutes or until sauce becomes the consistency of heavy cream. Add chopped basil and simmer another 2 to 3 minutes. Add salt and white pepper to taste.

In large kettle, cook the fettuccine in boiling, salted water with a tablespoon of oil. When it has reached the "al dente" stage (still firm to the bite), drain immediately.

Add the sauce to the hot fettuccine, toss and serve immediately on warm plates. Add a leaf or two of basil to each serving for garnish. Pass a bowl of freshly grated Parmesan cheese.   Serves 6 to 8.

Serve with Chardonnay.

Bow Tie Pasta with Chicken, Mushrooms and Artichokes

1 package (12 ounces) bow tie
  pasta
1 medium onion, finely
chopped
3 cloves garlic, minced
2 tablespoons olive oil
1 tablespoon minced
  oregano
1 tablespoon minced basil
2 cups sliced mushrooms

3 cans (8 ounces each)
  tomato sauce
6 slices prosciutto, finely sliced
1 can (14 ounces) quartered
  artichoke hearts (non-
  marinated)
½ cup half-and-half
4 grilled or baked skinless,
  boneless chicken breasts
Parmesan cheese

Cook pasta according to package directions. Cover and put aside. Keep warm.

Sauté onion and garlic in olive oil until soft; add herbs and mushrooms and sauté until mushrooms are lightly browned. Add tomato sauce, prosciutto and artichokes and simmer about 20 minutes.

Just before serving, add the half-and-half to the sauce. Slice chicken breasts. Top pasta with sauce, sliced chicken breasts and Parmesan cheese.   Serves 6.

Serve with Chardonnay.

Wild Mushroom Ravioli with White Truffle Oil

3 shallots, finely minced
2 tablespoons olive oil
1 pound wild mushrooms,
 chanterelles, oyster,
 cinnamon caps, porcini, etc.,
 cleaned and chopped
2 ounces Havarti cheese,
 grated
2 ounces Romano cheese,
 finely grated
3-4 ounces Mascarpone
 cheese

½ cup Marsala wine
Salt and pepper
Sheets of herbed pasta - use
 your favorite pasta recipe
 and add freshly chopped
 herbs, or buy ready-made
1 cup Madeira wine
1 ½ cups veal demi-glace
White truffle oil

To make the filling, sauté shallots in olive oil until clear and add mushrooms and cook until just done. Take off heat, cool and then add cheeses. Reduce Marsala to a glaze and add to mushrooms. Correct seasoning with salt and pepper to taste.

Lay out pasta sheets, place 1 heaping tablespoon of filling inside a 3-inch square, brush edges of pasta with egg wash, and cover with top sheet of pasta. Press air out gently and cut. Other shapes and designs work well, too. Dust lightly with flour and let sit 1 hour.

Meanwhile, to prepare the sauce, bring ½ cup of the Madeira and ¾ cup of the veal demi-glace to boil and reduce to glaze and caramelize a bit in pan. Watch carefully. Add remaining Madeira and veal demi-glace and thicken if necessary with arrowroot mixed with water. Check seasonings

Bring 3 to 4 quarts water to boil. Put in some of the raviolis (don't get too crowded) and turn down to barely a simmer. Cook 3 to 4 minutes to al dente.

Remove raviolis and mix with sauce, and then drizzle white truffle oil generously on top.   Serves 4.

Serve with Sauvignon Blanc.

Green Pasta with Herbs

A cool, flavorful dish for a warm evening or a summer luncheon.

1 pound fusilli noodles
2 tablespoons butter
2 tablespoons olive oil
4 cloves garlic, crushed
1 cup dry white wine

3 twists of a pepper grinder
1 tablespoon red chili powder
1 cup finely chopped mixed
   basil, mint and parsley
Grated Romano cheese

Cook the noodles until tender. Keep warm.

Melt the butter and olive oil in a large skillet. Add the garlic and cook over low heat until it begins to brown slightly. Add the wine and cook until liquid is reduced by half. Add the herbs. Toss with the pasta and serve with Romano cheese. Serves 4.

Serve with Sauvignon Blanc.

Fresh Basil and Tomatoes Pasta

1 ½ pounds ripe Roma
   tomatoes, coarsely
   chopped*
1 bunch basil leaves, sliced
   julienne
2 cloves fresh garlic, crushed
½ teaspoon crushed
   peppercorns

1 teaspoon salt
¼ teaspoon dried oregano
Pinch of crushed dried red
   chile peppers
1 pound pasta
Freshly grated Parmesan
   cheese

Combine the tomatoes, basil, garlic, peppercorns, salt, oregano and chili peppers in large bowl, cover. Let stand at room temperature for 1 hour. Cook pasta according to package directions. Remove from heat when al dente. Drain. To serve, top hot pasta with tomato mixture and sprinkle with Parmesan cheese. Serves 4 to 6.

Serve with a Zinfandel.

Fresh garden tomatoes may be substituted.

Fettuccini with Sun-Dried Tomatoes, California Prunes and Mustard

3 tablespoons chopped sun-dried tomatoes
4 large California pitted prunes, chopped
2 tablespoons mustard
2 tablespoons butter
1 tablespoon olive oil
⅓ cup chopped leeks (1 leek)
1 cup chopped fresh zucchini

1 tablespoon minced garlic
½ cup chopped fresh basil
¾ cup chopped wild mushrooms
4-5 ounces fettuccini pasta
2 tablespoons Zinfandel
½ cup chopped fresh parsley
½ cup chopped pecans

In a large pot, bring salted water to a boil in preparation for cooking pasta. Mix together the sun-dried tomatoes, chopped prunes and mustard. Set aside.

In sauté pan over medium heat, melt 1 tablespoon of the butter and oil together, and sauté the leeks and zucchini for 3 to 4 minutes. Add minced garlic and sauté for 30 seconds, then add basil and mushrooms; sauté for 1 minute before adding the tomato/prune mixture. Sauté for 1 to 2 minutes more. The pan will start to brown on the bottom. Remove vegetables and keep warm.

Begin cooking pasta. While pasta is cooking, add remaining 1 tablespoon of butter to sauté pan to loosen pan drippings; then splash pan with wine and deglaze. Return vegetables to pan to reheat and coat for several seconds; turn off heat. Quickly drain pasta and rinse under hot water; shake to remove all water, then toss with light coat of olive oil. Put pasta on hot plates and add fresh cracked black pepper and spoon vegetables on top. Sprinkle with fresh parsley and chopped pecans. Serve immediately.

Serves 2.

Serve with Zinfandel or a Syrah.

Pasta with Scallops in Lemon Herb Cream Sauce

2 teaspoons chopped fresh
   marjoram
½ cup butter
1 clove garlic, minced
2 shallots, finely minced
½ pound scallops

½ cup dry white wine
2 cups cream
1 tablespoon lemon zest
6-8 ounces (½ package)
   fettuccini pasta
½ teaspoon grated lemon zest

Wash, dry and chop the fresh marjoram; set aside.

Melt butter in non-corrosive saucepan and sauté garlic and shallots for two minutes or until golden. Add scallops and sauté, coating with butter. Add wine and poach for 3 to 5 minutes. Take care not to overcook or the scallops will toughen. Remove scallops and keep warm.

Reduce liquid by ⅓. Add cream, reduce for twenty minutes; however, during the last five minutes, add the marjoram and lemon zest, and stir until warmed through. Fold in scallops.

While the sauce is reducing, cook pasta until "just" done. Drain and rinse quickly with warm water. Shake out excess water. Coat with one or two tablespoons of olive oil. Toss with lemon zest.

Serve pasta topped with sauce and garnished with fresh herbs.
Serves 2.

Serve with Fumé Blanc.

Pappardelle with Sweet Red Peppers

Lovely fresh flavors combine for rave reviews on this dish.

6-8 sweet red peppers
2 medium onions, chopped
4 tablespoons olive oil
2 garlic cloves, finely chopped
1 tablespoon chopped fresh
  basil
1 cup beef or chicken stock

1 ½ pounds fresh pasta cut in
  wide strips, or 1 pound dried
  wide noodles
½ cup sun-dried tomatoes
  (packed in oil), chopped
½ cup toasted pine nuts

Char peppers on all sides, either over an open flame or under the broiler. Place still-hot peppers in a brown paper bag to steam for 5 minutes. When cool enough to handle, remove the charred skin, seeds and top. Chop the peppers coarsely. Reserve.

Sauté onion in 2 tablespoons of the olive oil until translucent. Add the chopped peppers, garlic and basil and the remaining oil; sauté a few minutes, then add stock. Cook over medium heat for 10 to 15 minutes until tender. Reserve a third of the mixture, purée the rest in a food processor.

Cook pasta in a large pot of boiling water until tender. Toss with the puréed pepper mixture. Fold in reserved pepper pieces and sun-dried tomatoes. Season to taste with salt and pepper. Garnish with toasted pine nuts and serve.   Serves 8.

Serve with Gamay Beaujolais.

Sweet
Pepper

95

Cheese Tortellini with a Pesto Cream Sauce and Grilled Chicken

1 cup tightly packed fresh basil leaves
1 clove garlic, minced
1 tablespoon extra virgin olive oil
4 walnut halves
1 tablespoon freshly grated Parmesan cheese
½ pound unsalted butter
1 pint heavy whipping cream
2 tablespoons olive oil (for pasta water)

1 tablespoon salt (for pasta water)
9-10 ounces fresh cheese tortellini
1 whole boneless, skinless chicken breast, grilled and sliced julienne
¼ yellow bell pepper, roasted, skinned and sliced julienne
¼ red bell pepper, roasted, skinned and sliced julienne

Make the pesto first by adding the following ingredients into a food processor: basil leaves, garlic, extra virgin olive oil, walnuts and Parmesan cheese. Process for 1 minute.

On the stove top in a medium saucepan, melt the unsalted butter. When melted, add the heavy whipping cream, whisking while it comes to a boil. Simmer for 5 minutes; then add the pesto sauce. Bring to a second boil and reduce heat to a simmer for 20 to 30 minutes, stirring occasionally.

In a large saucepan, bring 3 quarts of water to a boil with the olive oil and salt. Add tortellini and cook for 5 to 8 minutes, or until tender but firm. Drain the water and place the tortellini back in the same warm saucepan. Add the pesto cream sauce and the julienne chicken breast; toss gently. Divide into six portions and garnish with criss-crossed julienne red and yellow bell peppers.   Serves 6.

Serve with Fumé Blanc.

Zinfandel Noodles

6 egg yolks
2 whole eggs
¼ cup Zinfandel
2 teaspoons olive oil
¾ teaspoon salt

3 ½ cups flour (approximately)
½ cup melted butter
1 teaspoon chopped fresh
 rosemary

With a wire whisk, beat together the egg yolks, whole eggs, wine, oil and salt until well blended. Pour into flour. Mix with a heavy spoon until it begins to hold together. Turn out onto a floured board and knead until very smooth and elastic, about 10 minutes.

Cut into sixths and roll thin. Cut by hand or hand-operated noodle machine (following machine instructions). Let the cut noodles dry over a wooden stick for about 1 hour. You may then freeze individual portions on a cookie sheet and later store in a plastic bag in the freezer for future use. Makes about 8 cups cooked noodles.

To cook, bring at least 4 quarts of water to a boil. Add 1 tablespoon salt and olive oil. Drop noodles into rapidly boiling water and cook for 2 to 3 minutes. Drain well and serve with melted butter and chopped fresh rosemary.   Serves 6 to 8.

Serve with a Zinfandel.

Spaghetti al Fromaggio

1 pound ground beef
½ cup chopped onion
¼ cup chopped green pepper
1 small clove garlic, crushed
1 can (1 pound) tomatoes
1 can (6 ounces) tomato paste
1 teaspoon salt
½ teaspoon crushed basil
½ teaspoon crushed oregano

1 cup shredded Sonoma Jack
  cheese
¼ cup grated Sonoma Dry
  Jack cheese
1 package (7-8 ounces) thin
  spaghetti
Grated Sonoma Dry Jack
  cheese

Cook beef with onion, green pepper and garlic in large skillet until meat is browned. Stir in tomatoes, tomato paste, salt, basil and oregano. Simmer 30 minutes. Just before serving, stir in Sonoma Jack cheese and Sonoma Dry Jack cheese.

Meanwhile, prepare spaghetti according to package directions; drain. Turn spaghetti onto heated platter. Serve sauce over spaghetti with additional grated Dry Jack cheese. Serves 4 to 6.

Serve with a Merlot.

Saffron Risotto

4 tablespoons unsalted butter
½ onion, chopped
1 ⅔ cups Arborio rice
½ cup Chardonnay

Generous pinch of powdered
  saffron
4 cups low-salt chicken broth,
  heated

Melt butter in a heavy pan. Add onions and sauté until golden. Add rice and stir to coat all the grains with butter. Pour in the wine and cook, stirring until evaporated.

Dissolve saffron in a little of the hot broth and add to rice. Add remaining broth a little at a time, stirring often. You will need to regulate the heat to the point where the rice is just barely bubbling throughout this procedure. As soon as all the stock is incorporated into the rice, serve immediately. Serves 4.

Noodles with Minted Cucumber Sauce

6 ounces egg noodles
1 tablespoon olive oil
2 small cucumbers, peeled
  and chopped fine
4 green onions, thinly sliced
1 teaspoon minced fresh mint
  leaves

1 cup plain yogurt
2 tablespoons cream cheese
½ tablespoon flour
Salt and pepper
½ cup chopped toasted
  pecans

Cook noodles according to directions on package. Drain, set aside and keep warm. Heat olive oil in skillet. Cook cucumber, onions and mint for 2 to 3 minutes. In a bowl, mix yogurt, cream cheese and flour until cheese is blended into yogurt. Stir into cucumber mixture and heat until just hot (do not boil). Season to taste with salt and pepper. Toss with hot pasta. Sprinkle chopped pecans on top before serving.   Serves 4.

Serve with Sauvignon Blanc.

Fettuccini with Lemon Caper Sauce

1 package (6 ounces)
  fettuccini pasta
2 strips fresh lemon peel
2 garlic cloves, crushed
8 tablespoons butter
½ cup Chardonnay wine

1 tablespoon lemon juice
2 tablespoons capers
2 tablespoon minced fresh basil
¼ cup grated Parmesan cheese
2 tablespoons minced fresh
  parsley

Place pasta in boiling water, to which you have added the lemon peel strips. Cook according to package directions. Drain and discard lemon.

Sauté garlic in the butter until slightly browned. Remove garlic and discard. Stir in wine, lemon juice, capers, and basil. Heat just until hot. Toss with hot pasta. Add Parmesan cheese and toss well. Sprinkle with parsley before serving.   Serves 4

Serve with a crispy green salad and a chilled Chardonnay.

Linguini with Clams Monterey

1 large onion, diced
3 cloves garlic, minced
¼ cup olive oil
½ cup chopped parsley
1 cup sliced fresh mushrooms
2 tablespoons chopped fresh
    basil (or 1 teaspoon
    dried)
¼ cup dry white wine

2 cans (6 ½ ounces each)
    minced or chopped clams
½ tablespoon chopped fresh
    oregano
Dash cayenne
Salt and pepper
¼ cup freshly grated
    Parmesan cheese
1 pound linguini

Sauté onions and garlic in olive oil over medium-high heat in heavy sauté pan until golden. Add chopped parsley, mushrooms and basil. Sauté for approximately 3 minutes until blended. Splash white wine into mixture and simmer until reduced by 1/2. Add clams with their juices, the oregano and cayenne. Season to taste with salt and pepper.

After mixture has returned to a simmer, stir in Parmesan and continue to simmer, uncovered. Prepare pasta according to package directions in boiling water, with 1 tablespoon olive oil. Cook until al dente.

Drain pasta and add clam mixture. Sprinkle liberally with grated Parmesan or Asiago cheese, and serve. Serves 6 to 8.

This is especially good served with a green salad, crusty sourdough bread and a chilled Sauvignon Blanc.

Spaghetti Primavera

1 pound hot Italian sausage
4 tablespoons oil
2 cloves garlic, minced
1 can (28 ounces) Italian plum
  tomatoes, drained and
  chopped
1 cup finely chopped parsley
1 sprig fresh oregano (or 1
  teaspoon dried)
Salt and ground black pepper

1 pound dried Italian spaghettini
½ pound tender, young
  zucchini, thinly sliced
3 red bell peppers, seeded
  and thinly sliced
½ pound fresh snow peas,
  cleaned and washed
¼ cup chopped fresh basil
¾ cup freshly grated
  Parmesan cheese

In a pot, cover sausages with water. Boil until cooked, about 30 minutes. Remove, peel and slice thinly. Heat 2 tablespoons of the oil in heavy skillet over medium heat. Add sausage and brown. Remove. Discard all but 2 tablespoons of fat from skillet.

Add garlic and sauté until transparent — do not brown. Add tomatoes, ¾ cup of the parsley, oregano, salt and pepper to taste. Cover and simmer gently for 15 minutes. Watch carefully, and stir from time to time. Add a little water if it gets too dry. Add sausage, cover and keep warm.

Cook the spaghettini according to package directions.

Meanwhile, in another skillet, add the remaining 2 tablespoons of the oil and heat to medium high. Dry the snow peas on paper towels. Add the zucchini and red bell peppers to the skillet and sauté a few minutes. Then add the snow peas and cook until they turn bright green. Add the vegetables to the sauce and toss thoroughly with the pasta and basil.

Sprinkle with remaining ¼ cup of the parsley and Parmesan. Pass additional Parmesan cheese and serve with French bread.

Serves 6 to 8.

Serve with Cabernet Sauvignon.

Polenta with Italian Sausage

4 sweet red peppers, coarsely
  chopped
2 medium onions, coarsely
  chopped
4 cloves garlic, minced
4 medium zucchini, cubed
½ cup roughly chopped fresh
  basil leaves

Salt and pepper
8 mild or hot Italian sausages
1 cup red or white wine
2 cups coarse stone-ground
  yellow cornmeal or polenta
  flour
1 tablespoon butter

Place the peppers, onions, garlic and zucchini into a large roasting pan. Add the basil leaves, and salt and pepper to taste. Place the sausages on top of the vegetables and puncture them several times with a fork. Roast in a 425 degree oven for 30 to 40 minutes, or until done. Deglaze the pan with the wine and hold in a warm oven.

Bring 4 cups of water to a boil, add the polenta a little at a time, whisking continually. When you have added all the polenta, add butter, then lower the heat and continue stirring until the mixture has thickened, about 10 minutes. Pour polenta into a bowl or onto a wooden platter. For even creamier polenta, fold in a few ¼-inch slices of Teleme Jack cheese as it begins to thicken.

Serve polenta topped with the sausage and vegetable mixture.

Serves 6.

Serve with a Merlot.

Italian Rice Torta

2 cups cooked rice
4 eggs
2 heaping tablespoons finely
  chopped basil and parsley

2 cloves garlic, finely chopped
½ cup Parmesan cheese
½ cup white wine
Salt and pepper

Combine ingredients and bake 30 to 40 minutes at 350 degrees. For variations, add 1 cup chopped and cooked green onions or leeks, broccoli, French cut green beans or celery.   Serves 6 to 8.

California Rice

A delicious rice dish, equally good with poultry or pork.

1 cup short grain brown rice
2 cups chicken stock
1 cup Riesling or Chenin Blanc
1 teaspoon salt
3 tablespoons butter
¾ cup dried apricots, slivered
¾ cup quartered pitted prunes
1 cup chopped celery

1 cup chopped onion
2 teaspoons crumbled dried
  sweet basil
½ teaspoon crumbled thyme
¾ cup coarsely chopped
  walnuts, lightly toasted
¼ cup chopped parsley

In a 3-quart saucepan with a tight-fitting lid, combine rice, chicken stock, ½ cup of the wine, salt and 1 of the tablespoon butter. Bring to a boil. Lower heat until liquid is just simmering. Cover and simmer about 1 hour without removing lid. When liquid has evaporated, remove from heat and allow to steam, covered, for 10 to 15 minutes. Fluff rice with fork.

Meanwhile, place apricots in small pot. Top with prunes and the remaining ½ cup of the wine, and bring to a boil. Remove from heat and set aside to cool. Melt the remaining 2 tablespoons of the butter in skillet. Add celery, onions, basil and thyme. Sauté over medium heat for 5 minutes. Add to rice, along with cooled fruits, walnuts and parsley. Toss well to combine. Spoon into buttered baking dish, cover, and heat in 325 degree oven for 30 minutes before serving.

Serves 8.

Serve with Riesling or Chenin Blanc.

Meats

THE HERBS & SPICES COOKBOOK

Grilled Butterflied Leg of Lamb

⅔ cup Shoyu Sauce (or low-
    salt soy sauce)
1 tablespoon Herbes de
    Provence*

1 boneless, butterflied leg of
    lamb (about 4 to 5 pounds)

To make the marinade, combine the Shoyu Sauce and Herbes de Provence. Place the lamb in a glass dish and pour marinade over it. Place in the refrigerator for twelve hours, turning the lamb from time to time to ensure it is well marinated. It may be left as long as 24 hours.

Remove the lamb from the refrigerator approximately 1 hour before grilling. Drain the lamb, but save the marinade.

Prepare mesquite coals (combine with grapevine or applewood cuttings if they are available). When coals are sufficiently hot, grill the lamb approximately 5 inches from the coals for 20 minutes per side. Baste frequently with marinade. When done, remove onto a warm plate and let stand 10 minutes prior to serving.

Serve with your favorite red potato or pasta salad and a Merlot.

Serves 8.

An aromatic blend of thyme, summer savory, basil, rosemary and lavender.

Minted Grilled Lamb

½ cup firmly-packed parsley sprigs

½ cup firmly-packed fresh mint leaves

4 large cloves garlic, peeled and halved

4 green onions (including tops) cut into 1-inch pieces

2 tablespoons fresh lemon juice

2 tablespoons raspberry vinegar or red wine vinegar

½ teaspoon crushed dried thyme

¼ teaspoon crushed dried rosemary

¼ teaspoon pepper

⅓ cup olive oil

1 leg of lamb (about 5 pounds) boned and butterflied, or 6 to 8 lamb steaks, cut 1-inch thick

Place parsley, mint, garlic, green onions, lemon juice, vinegar, thyme, rosemary and pepper in a food processor or blender. Process until finely chopped. With motor running, slowly add olive oil to make a smooth paste. Rub marinade on all sides of lamb. Place lamb in a bowl, cover and refrigerate for 2 hours or overnight.

To cook, place lamb on a lightly greased grill, about 4 inches above a solid bed of low-glowing coals. Cook, turning occasionally, until lamb is well browned, but still pink in the center when cut. Allow about 50 minutes for leg, 12 to 15 minutes for steaks.

Makes 6 to 8 servings.

Serve with Cabernet Sauvignon.

Lamb with Cilantro-Cumin Crust

2 whole lamb loins
Olive oil
Salt

½ bunch cilantro, stemmed
2 tablespoons ground cumin
½ teaspoon cayenne pepper

Clean the loins of all fat and silverskin. If the tenderloins are attached, clean them as well. Brush with olive oil and sprinkle with salt.

Purée the cilantro leaves in a food processor with the cumin and cayenne. Add olive oil a tablespoon at a time until mixture is the consistency of jam. Smear over the loins and set aside, covered, for ½ to 1 hour. (They may also be held overnight, refrigerated.)

Prepare a charcoal fire or preheat a gas grill.

Grill the loins for approximately 4 minutes per side for rare. (Times are approximate due to the variability of grill temperatures.) Meat should spring back to the touch, or use the sharp point of a knife to test for desired doneness. The smaller tenderloins will, of course, cook more quickly.

Let meat rest for a few minutes, then cut into slices and arrange on warmed plates.
                                                    Serves 4.

Serve with Sauvignon Blanc.

Mushroom Beef Stew

Flour
Salt and pepper
2 pounds boneless beef
  chuck, cut into 1 ½-inch
  cubes
3 tablespoons olive or other
  vegetable oil
2 medium onions, sliced thin
1 clove garlic, minced
2 cups dry red wine
1 cup beef stock or canned
  broth

3 tablespoons chopped fresh
  parsley
1 ½ teaspoons oregano
½ teaspoon thyme
1 bay leaf
2 slices bacon, chopped
2 fresh tomatoes, chopped
1 pound mushrooms, cut in
  thick slices
2 tablespoons butter
Fresh parsley for garnish

Place flour on plate, season with salt and pepper. Coat beef with flour, shaking off excess. Heat the oil in heavy, large Dutch oven over high heat. Brown beef a few pieces at a time, browning well on all sides.

Return beef and any accumulated juices to Dutch oven. Reduce heat to medium. Add onion and garlic; cook for 1 minute. Add wine and enough beef stock to cover meat. Add parsley, oregano, thyme, and bay leaf. Cover and bake in a 325 degree oven for about 2 hours.

Heat a frying pan and cook bacon until crisp. Transfer to paper towel to drain. Add chopped tomatoes to pan and sauté 5 minutes. Add bacon and tomatoes to Dutch oven. Thin liquid with wine, if necessary. Cover and bake approximately 30 more minutes or until meat is tender.

Sauté mushrooms in butter until tender. Add to stew just before serving. Season with salt and pepper to taste, and garnish with fresh parsley.   Serves 4 to 6.

Serve with Cabernet Sauvignon.

Estofado
Mediterranean Stew

3 pounds very lean stew meat
  (tri-tip or sirloin)
¼ cup olive oil
2 large onions, thinly sliced
1 large clove of garlic, minced
  or pressed
1 bay leaf
2 tablespoons dried currants
6 ounces tomato paste
2 tablespoons wine vinegar

½ cup Zinfandel or dry red
  table wine
1 tablespoon brown sugar
¼ teaspoon ground cinnamon
½ teaspoon ground cumin
⅛ teaspoon ground cloves
½ pound feta cheese
3/4-1 cup walnut halves
Salt and pepper

Cut meat into 1 ½-inch cubes. Heat the olive oil in a large frying pan until hot. Brown meat on all sides for 5 minutes on high heat. Stir to avoid sticking or scorching. Add onions and garlic and continue stirring for 5 minutes, until coated with oil. Add bay leaf, currants, tomato paste, vinegar, wine, brown sugar, cinnamon, cumin and cloves.

Cover, reduce heat to low and simmer for 2 hours, until meat is tender and sauce is thick. Stir occasionally to prevent sticking. Just before serving, stir in cheese and walnuts. Serve with rice or noodles.

                                      Serves 6 to 8.

Suggested wine: Cabernet Sauvignon or Petit Syrah.

Braised Beef Ragout with Sage Pappardelle and Roasted Garlic Cabernet Sauce

4 pounds rump roast or round
  steak
1 large carrot, sliced
2 medium onions, sliced
½ celery stalk, sliced
4 garlic cloves
2 shallots, sliced
1 bay leaf
4 sprigs thyme
6 peppercorns
2 whole cloves

2 parsley stems
6 cups Cabernet Sauvignon
1 cup vinegar
4 ounces pork rind (trimmed of
  all fat and blanched)
3 cups good brown stock
Small Bouquet Garni
Salt and pepper
2 tablespoons mashed roasted
  garlic
Oil

Cut the beef into 2-inch cubes. Divide carrots, onions, celery, garlic, shallots, bay leaf, thyme, peppercorns, cloves and parsley into 2 parts. Place half on the bottom of a stainless steel container, then place the beef, followed by the other half of the vegetables and herbs. Pour wine and the vinegar over to cover. Refrigerate for 12 hours to marinate, turning the meat a couple of times.

Remove beef from marinade and pat dry; reserve the marinade. Sear the beef in oil on top of the stove until a caramelized crust of juices has formed. Set the pieces of meat aside. When this has been done, strain the vegetables and herbs from the reserved marinade, keeping the liquid. Sauté the vegetables in the same pan as the beef, then pour in the liquid from the marinade and reduce by ⅔, releasing the sediments from the bottom of the pan with a wooden spoon.

Pour the vegetables into a thick pot just big enough to hold the ingredients. Place the pork rind on the vegetables and add the pieces of beef. Barely cover the meat with the brown stock and bring to a boil. Add the Bouquet Garni and season with salt and pepper. Cover pot with foil leaving no gaps between meat and foil. Cover with pot lid. Braise in a 325 degree oven for 1 ½ to 2 hours.

Remove pieces of beef to a clean pot; the stock should have reduced to a good consistency while cooking; if not, and remains somewhat thin, reduce it quickly until it coats the back of a spoon.

Strain the stock over the beef adding the mashed roasted garlic, and correct the seasoning with salt and pepper to taste. At this point you may add some blanched baby vegetables (i.e., carrots, turnips, pearl onions, etc.,) or a mixture of sautéed wild mushrooms.

SAGE PAPPARDELLE NOODLES:

1 whole egg (at room temperature)	½ cup sage leaves
	1 teaspoon salt
2 egg yolks (at room temperature)	1 ¼ cups unbleached all-purpose flour

Blend egg and yolks in a blender with the sage leaves. Sieve flour and salt onto a table top. Make a well in the center adding about 80% of the egg and sage mixture to the well. In a circular motion with your fingertips, gradually incorporate the flour into the egg mixture. When a paste is formed, you may push most of the flour over the paste leaving any you may think you won't need.

With both hands, knead the dough into a crumbly mass. If too dry, place a little egg mixture into the palm of your hand and carry on kneading. Knead the dough for about 12 minutes, so your dough is able to stretch without difficulty. Rest the dough, covered, for about 30 minutes before cutting the dough following the instructions for your machine.

The Sage Pappardelle Noodles should be approximately 1 by 3 ½ inches. Cook in boiling salted water, approximately 3 minutes until tender.

Toss the noodles in seasoned olive oil before placing onto a serving platter under the braised beef.   Serves 6 to 8.

Serve with a Cabernet Sauvignon.

Grilled Steak Provencal

4 fillet mignon or New York
   steaks (6 to 8 ounces each)
2 tablespoons olive oil
Salt and pepper
2 large cloves garlic, minced
1 medium onion, thinly sliced
⅓ cup Cabernet Sauvignon,
   Merlot or Zinfandel

½ cup chicken broth
1 cup chopped fresh tomatoes
½ cup thinly sliced, pitted
   Greek style olives
½ teaspoon crumbled dried
   rosemary
½ teaspoon dried oregano

Start your grill. Rub both sides of each steak with 1 tablespoon of the oil, then sprinkle with salt and pepper. Grill steaks to desired doneness.

Meanwhile, heat the remaining tablespoon of oil in a heavy skillet over medium-high heat; add garlic and onions. Sauté until onions are tender. Add the wine, chicken broth, tomatoes, olives, rosemary and oregano. Increase heat under skillet to high; boil sauce until slightly thickened. Spoon sauce over each steak.   Serves 4.

Serve with Cabernet Sauvignon or Merlot.

Vintner's Stew

4 ounces bacon, chopped (4-5 slices)
2 large onions, coarsely chopped (about 3 cups)
4-6 tablespoons olive oil
½ cup flour
1 teaspoon salt
1 teaspoon freshly ground pepper
3 pounds chuck or cross rib beef, cut into 2-inch cubes
1 ½ cups Cabernet Sauvignon
1 cup beef broth
1 can (8 ounces) tomato sauce

1 large bay leaf
½ teaspoon crumbled dried thyme
2 large garlic cloves, minced
1 tablespoon Worcestershire sauce
½ ounce unsweetened chocolate, chopped
18 boiling onions, peeled
1 ½ pounds carrots, peeled and cut into 2-inch lengths
¾ pound small fresh mushrooms

In a large, heavy pot with a tight-fitting lid, sauté bacon until all fat is rendered. Remove crisp bacon bits. Cook chopped onion in bacon fat over medium-high heat, stirring often, until dark brown, at least 30 minutes. Remove onions and add 2 tablespoons of oil to the pot. Place flour, salt and pepper in small bag. Add beef cubes a few at a time and shake to coat well. Brown meat in small batches (don't crowd the pot), adding more oil as needed. Transfer meat to bowl after browning. Add wine and broth to pot. Bring to a boil over high heat, scraping up any brown bits on bottom and sides of pot. Add tomato sauce, bay leaf, thyme, garlic, Worcestershire sauce, bacon bits, browned onions and meat. Stir well and return to a boil. Lower heat, cover tightly and simmer 30 minutes. Stir every 15 minutes throughout 1 ½ hours of cooking time. Add chocolate, stirring until dissolved. Stir in small onions, cover and simmer 30 minutes. Add carrots and mushrooms. Cover and cook for another 30 minutes.   Serves 6.

Serve with boiled red-skinned potatoes (unpeeled) tossed with chopped parsley, a crisp green salad, and a Cabernet Sauvignon.

Alternate serving suggestion: Serve in individual round French bread loaves. Slice top from each small loaf and hollow out the center, leaving a 3/4-inch thick shell. Spoon stew into bread shells. Replace tops, slightly off center. Serve this with a crisp green salad.

Baked Cranberry Pork Chops

4 loin pork chops (1 ½ to 2
  pounds)
1 tablespoon vegetable oil
1 medium onion, sliced fine
1 can (16 ounces) jellied
  cranberry sauce
2 tablespoons light brown
  sugar

1 teaspoon ground ginger
⅛ teaspoon ground nutmeg
2 cups fresh carrots, cut in thin
  strips (julienned)
1 teaspoon cornstarch
1 tablespoon chopped fresh
  parsley

Brown pork chops in the oil along with the sliced onion. Set aside.
Preheat oven to 375 degrees.

In a medium saucepan, heat cranberry sauce, 2 tablespoons water,
brown sugar, ginger and nutmeg until cranberry sauce is melted,
about 2 minutes. Place carrots in a 2 1/2-quart casserole. Arrange
pork chops over carrots. Spoon cranberry sauce mixture evenly
over pork chops. Cover and bake until pork is thoroughly cooked,
about 45 minutes to 1 hour.

Remove chops to a serving plate. Scatter carrots over chops. Pour
sauce remaining in casserole into a medium saucepan. Combine
cornstarch with 1 tablespoon water; stir into saucepan. Cook and
stir until sauce is clear and thickened, about 2 minutes. Spoon over
pork chops. Sprinkle with chopped parsley.   Serves 4.

Serve with a Zinfandel.

Basil Pork Chops Barbera

3 tablespoons olive oil
4 center cut pork chops, 1-inch
thick
½ pound fresh mushrooms,
sliced
1 cup sliced green onions
¼ cup chopped fresh basil

Salt and freshly ground pepper
8 large cloves garlic, chopped
½ cup Barbera wine
1 can (28 ounces) plum
tomatoes, drained and
crushed (reserve juice)
¼ cup chopped fresh parsley

In a heavy skillet, heat oil to medium temperature. Score edges of chops to prevent curling. Quickly brown chops on both sides. Remove to a plate, and set aside.

Lower heat, add sliced mushrooms, green onions, basil, salt and pepper. Stir and sauté for 2 minutes. Add chopped garlic and wine to deglaze pan. Add crushed tomatoes and mix well.

Return chops with accumulated juice to skillet and spoon sauce over. Simmer uncovered for 45 minutes and sauce is reduced. Add reserved tomato liquid as needed to adjust sauce. Add chopped parsley 5 minutes before cooking time is completed.   Serves 4.

Serve with Merlot or Zinfandel.

Roasted Rack of Lamb with Cabernet Rosemary Tangerine Sauce

1 crown lamb rack, frenched and trimmed (about 8 chops)
Salt and pepper
2 tablespoons finely chopped fresh rosemary
2 tablespoons finely chopped fresh thyme
2 tablespoons finely chopped fresh parsley
2 tablespoons finely chopped fresh mint
2 tablespoons finely chopped fresh basil
1 tablespoon tangerine zest
1 tablespoon Dijon mustard
2 tablespoons olive oil
¼ cup Brandy
4 cloves garlic, coarsely chopped
½ cup Cabernet Sauvignon
2 ounces rich lamb stock (or beef stock)
Fresh rosemary to garnish

Rub lamb with salt and pepper, herbs, tangerine zest and mustard. Let set overnight, or at least 6 hours.

Sear lamb in olive oil, meat side down, until golden brown. Deglaze with Brandy. Add garlic and turn lamb over until it rests on bones. Roast in oven until rare (450 degrees for about 20 to 30 minutes).

TANGERINE SAUCE:
½ cup honey
2 tablespoons finely chopped mint
¼ cup Dijon mustard
¼ cup grain mustard
Additional tangerine zest
Salt and pepper
1 tablespoon butter, cut into pieces

While meat is roasting, make the Tangerine Sauce by mixing honey, mint, mustards, zest, salt and pepper to taste, and butter.

When lamb is ready, remove from pan and pour off excess grease. Deglaze with wine, let reduce. Add lamb stock and again reduce down. Add the Tangerine Sauce and stir thoroughly, adding pieces of butter until smooth. Keep warm. Arrange lamb chops on prepared dish and drizzle sauce over lamb. Garnish with fresh rosemary and tangerine rind twists. Accompany with oven-braised fennel or fennel purée.
                                                                 Serves 4.

Serve with Cabernet Sauvignon.

Roast Leg of Lamb with Pesto Pine Nut Filling

¾ cup olive oil
2 cups firmly packed basil
2 teaspoons minced garlic
2 teaspoons dried rosemary
1 teaspoon salt

½ teaspoon pepper
1 cup fresh bread crumbs
¼ cup pine nuts
1 leg of lamb (5-6 pounds)
   boned and butterflied

Preheat oven to 425 degrees. In a food processor, blend the olive oil, basil, garlic, rosemary, salt, and pepper until well blended. Reserve 2 teaspoons of this pesto mixture. Next, add the bread crumbs and then the pine nuts to the food processor. Process until just blended. Spread the filling evenly over the lamb. Roll the lamb, tucking in the ends and tie securely with string. Rub the outside with the reserved pesto.

Place lamb in shallow roasting pan and roast for about 1 hour. (For rare meat, cook 12 minutes per pound, 135 degrees on a meat thermometer; for medium, allow 15 minutes per pound, about 150 degrees on meat thermometer.)

Allow lamb to rest 15 minutes before carving (internal temperature will rise 5 to 10 degrees). Cut into ½-inch thick slices and serve.

Serves 8 to 10.

Serve with a Merlot.

Braised Rabbit with Sweet Potatoes, Lentils, and Meyer Lemon, Garlic and Green Beans

1 dressed rabbit
3 tablespoons peanut oil
1 large onion, quartered
1 carrot, cut in half
1 head garlic, cut in half
3 stalks celery

Several large sprigs rosemary
3 sprigs fresh sage
3 sprigs fresh thyme
2 cups Fumé Blanc
2-3 cups water
Salt and freshly ground pepper

To prepare the rabbit, cut it into 8 pieces. Salt and sear in small amount of peanut oil until well browned. Pour off oil, return rabbit to pan and add quartered onion, carrot, garlic, celery, rosemary, sage and thyme. Add Fumé Blanc and water (just enough to barely cover rabbit). Simmer for about 1 hour. Meanwhile, prepare the vegetables.

1 small sweet potato
1 small white onion, diced
½ pound lentils
3 cups vegetable stock
2 sprigs thyme
Salt

1 pound haricots verts, or
   tender Blue Lake beans
1 head garlic, cut in half
¼ cup extra virgin olive oil
2 Meyer lemons, quartered

Dice the sweet potatoes and white onion; rinse the lentils. Cook lentils in 3 times their volume of vegetable stock and water with sweet potatoes, onion and several sprigs of thyme for about 30 minutes. Season to taste with salt. Snip off stem ends of green beans leaving the tips natural. Blanch several minutes in boiling water, then refresh with ice water to set and retain their bright green color. Cook just before serving in olive oil with the head of garlic (cut in half) and quartered Meyer lemons. Season with salt to taste.

Remove rabbit from cooking liquid, strain and pour back over the rabbit (you can reduce it a bit first if you like). Serve rabbit and natural sauce over the vegetable mixture. Garnish with green beans, a cooked Meyer lemon wedge and a rosemary or sage sprig.
                                                                    Serves 6.

Enjoy with Cabernet Sauvignon.

Fricassee of Rabbit with Wild Mushrooms

1 rabbit, cut into eight pieces
1 tablespoon fresh thyme
leaves
Salt and freshly ground black
pepper
Olive oil, as needed
3 tablespoons Brandy
2 large cloves garlic, minced
2 bay leaves
½ cup Chardonnay

1 cup reduced veal stock, or
low-salt chicken broth
1 cup crème fraîche or heavy
whipping cream
1 pound wild mushrooms,
sliced
Unsalted butter, as needed
2 tablespoons chopped Italian
parsley

Sprinkle rabbit with thyme, salt and pepper. Sauté in hot oil until golden brown. Remove rabbit from pan and pour off oil.

Return rabbit to pan. Add Brandy, stand back, and ignite! When flames die down, add garlic, bay leaves, wine, stock and crème fraîche. Simmer, covered, for approximately 1 hour or until rabbit is very tender.

While the rabbit is cooking, sauté the mushrooms in a little butter. Add to the rabbit during the last 10 minutes of cooking. Arrange the fricassee on a platter and garnish with chopped parsley. Serves 4.

Suggested wine: Chardonnay.

Spicy Tangine of Lamb with Apples

Pinch of saffron
Salt and pepper
1 scant teaspoon ground
  ginger
¼ teaspoon cinnamon
3 tablespoons grated onion
4-5 sprigs coriander leaves
  (cilantro)
2 tablespoons sweet butter,
  melted
2 tablespoons vegetable
  oil

3 to 3 ½ pounds shoulder of
  lamb or beef chuck in 1 ½-
  inch cubes
1 pound dried pitted prunes or
  apricots
1 cup finely sliced onions
½ teaspoon cinnamon
4 tablespoons honey
4 tart apples
1 tablespoon butter
1 tablespoon toasted sesame
  seeds

Mix the saffron, salt and pepper, ginger, cinnamon, onion and coriander with the butter and oil. Dip each lamb cube in butter mixture and place in casserole.

In a Dutch oven, cook lamb over low heat, turning and being careful not to burn them while allowing aroma of spices to be released. Cover meat with water, bring to boil, then lower heat. Simmer 1 hour.

Meanwhile, soak prunes in 2 cups cold water. After one hour, add prunes, onions, ¼ teaspoon of the cinnamon and 3 tablespoons of the honey to meat. Simmer uncovered until prunes swell and sauce has reduced to 1 cup.

Shortly before ready to serve, quarter and core apples. Sauté in skillet with the butter, remaining tablespoon of honey, and the remaining ¼ teaspoon cinnamon until soft and glazed.

To serve, arrange meat on dish, pour onion-prune sauce over, decorate with apples and sprinkle with toasted sesame seeds. Serve with couscous or rice.   Serves 8.

Serve with Cabernet or Zinfandel.

A Classic Chili

6 pounds top sirloin, trimmed
    and cubed into ½-inch
    pieces
Salt and pepper
1 cup olive oil
1 ½ large onions, chopped
2 jalapeños, seeded and diced
2 tablespoons chili powder
2 tablespoons paprika
1 tablespoon cumin
1 tablespoon cayenne

1 tablespoon coriander
1 bottle Cabernet Sauvignon
1 quart chicken stock
15 pear tomatoes, peeled and
    seeded, or 1 can (#10)
    peeled tomatoes with juice
5 chipotle peppers, diced
1 ½ tablespoons chopped
    garlic
2 cups fresh corn

Salt and pepper the beef. Heat 2 tablespoons of oil at a time in a thick-bottomed stock pot. Brown the beef in 3 batches, using more olive oil each time. Add 4 tablespoons of oil, the onions and jalapeños. Lightly brown the onions. Add the chili powder, paprika, cumin, cayenne and coriander. Lower the heat. Cook, stirring, for about 3 to 4 minutes.

Add the wine, stock, tomatoes, browned beef, chipotle peppers and garlic. Simmer until beef is tender, approximately 2 to 3 hours. Skim the top regularly. Garnish with corn. Serve with spoon bread and crème fraîche.
                                   Makes one gallon.

Wine suggestion: A hearty Cabernet Sauvignon.

Harvest Stew

4 tablespoons olive oil
¾ cup salt pork, diced
8 tablespoons butter
2 carrots, coarsely chopped
1 leek, coarsely chopped
4 shallots, coarsely chopped
1 large onion, coarsely
  chopped
1 clove garlic, minced
3 pounds beef (top round or
  rump) cut in large cubes
White flour

4 tablespoons Cognac,
  warmed
2 cups red wine
2 cups beef stock
Bouquet Garni
18 small onions, coarsely
  chopped
1 tablespoon sugar
12 mushroom caps
1 tablespoon lemon juice
fresh parsley, chopped

Put 2 tablespoons of the olive oil in skillet and sauté pork. Remove and set aside. In same skillet add 4 tablespoons of the butter to the oil and sauté vegetables. Remove and place with pork. Lightly flour beef and add another 2 tablespoons olive oil to skillet. Brown beef. Remove and add to sautéed items.

Pour warmed Cognac into a hot skillet and light. After the flame dies, mix all sautéed items in skillet and transfer to a 4-quart casserole dish. Pour all but 4 tablespoons red wine over ingredients and then add hot beef stock to cover. Add Bouquet Garni to casserole.

Cook slowly in a 280 to 300 degree oven for 1½ to 2 hours. Stir and continue to cook 2 hours longer. Remove Bouquet Garni. Add more wine if necessary.

Brown and caramelize small onions in 2 tablespoons of the butter and sugar. Add the remaining 4 tablespoons red wine and cook in covered skillet until almost tender. Sauté mushrooms in remaining 2 tablespoons butter and the lemon juice. Keep warm. When meat is tender, add onions and mushrooms and sprinkle lavishly with fresh, chopped parsley.   Serves 6 to 8.

Serve a simple salad with a vinaigrette dressing, crusty French bread and Merlot or Syrah with this stew.

Carneros Lamb

1 cup Pinot Noir
1 cup light soy sauce
½ cup olive oil
¼ cup coarse mustard
Zest of lemon
Handful of rosemary

Handful of oregano
Handful of mint
1 tablespoon cracked pepper
1 teaspoon sea salt
1 leg of lamb (3 pounds)

Have the butcher butterfly the leg of lamb, making sure that the thickest parts are not more than 2 inches thick. If using fresh herbs, coarsely chop (or cut the herbs with scissors) into 1-inch chunks.

To make the marinade, put the wine, soy sauce, oil, mustard, lemon zest, rosemary, oregano, mint, pepper and salt in a large bowl. Place the lamb in the bowl fat side up, so that the meat is in contact with the juices. Refrigerate; marinate for at least 4 hours, preferably overnight.

Strain and reserve the marinade. Reduce marinade over high heat while the lamb is cooking. Grill the lamb over a hot fire, turning several times, until done but still pink. Let rest 15 minutes before carving. Add any meat juices to the reduced marinade.

Serve lamb with mixed grilled vegetables, and the reduced marinade.   Serves 4 to 6.

Serve with a Pinot Noir.

Loin of Pork Patties with Blackberry Salsa

1 pound lean ground loin of pork
1 cup crushed cracker crumbs
½ teaspoon salt
½ teaspoon black pepper
2 teaspoons dried thyme

2 tablespoons prepared Dijon mustard
2 eggs, beaten
4 tablespoons butter
Blackberry Salsa (recipe follows)

Mix pork, cracker crumbs, salt, pepper, thyme, mustard, and eggs. Shape into 4 patties.

Heat butter in a large frying pan over medium heat. Add the patties and brown on both sides for about 15 minutes, turning occasionally. Serve with Blackberry Salsa.   Serves 4.

BLACKBERRY SALSA:
2 tablespoons olive oil
1 cup minced sweet onions
1 cup blackberries (fresh or frozen)

1 tablespoon sugar
½ cup Merlot
2 teaspoons finely chopped fresh mint

Heat olive oil in saucepan over medium heat. Sauté onions for 2 to 3 minutes, stirring, until onions become soft. Add blackberries and sugar, mashing slightly until fruit is blended with onion. Add wine and simmer for 10 minutes. Add mint. Serve warm.

Nutmeg mashed potatoes, peas with onions, a simple green salad, and Merlot will make this a special meal.

Spicy Plum Pork

2 pounds pork shoulder, trimmed and cut into 2-inch cubes
2 cups dry red wine, such as Merlot
1 ½ cups cooked fresh plum compote, or 1 can (16 ounces) plums, including juice, diced
10 dried apricots, diced

1 teaspoon allspice
3 cloves
1 bay leaf
½ teaspoon freshly grated nutmeg
¼ teaspoon cinnamon
¼ teaspoon cayenne pepper
2-inch piece fresh ginger, minced
3 cloves garlic, minced

Dredge the pork in flour seasoned with salt and pepper. Sear in hot oil in a large heavy Dutch oven. Add the remaining ingredients and bring to a simmer. Cover and place in a 350 degree oven for 2 hours. Serve with basmati rice and roasted carrots. Serves 4.

Serve with Merlot.

Herb Marinated Lamb Chops

4 lamb chops, well trimmed
⅓ cup dry red wine
2 tablespoons spicy mustard
Juice of 2 tangerines
½ teaspoon salt
1 tablespoon cracked black pepper

2 tablespoons minced chives
1 teaspoon chopped fresh rosemary
1 teaspoon chopped fresh thyme
½ teaspoon red pepper flakes

Place lamb chops in a heavy dish. Mix remaining ingredients and pour over lamb, turning to coat. Marinate at room temperature for least 1 hour.

Broil or grill the lamb chops to desired doneness. Serve on hot plates with asparagus, green beans or broccoli. Serves 2.

A Cabernet Sauvignon is suggested for this dish.

Poultry

THE HERBS & SPICES COOKBOOK

Sautéed Chicken & Grapes
In a Creamy Gingered Wine Sauce

4 skinless, boneless chicken
   breasts
1 cup Chardonnay
2 tablespoons minced fresh
   ginger
1 clove garlic, minced
2 green onions, sliced
1 teaspoon Dijon mustard

½ teaspoon salt
½ teaspoon black pepper
2 tablespoons olive oil
2 cups seedless green grapes
3 tablespoons cream cheese
½ package (8 ounces) egg
   noodles

Cut chicken breasts into ¾ -inch strips. Marinate in a mixture of the wine, ginger, garlic, onions, mustard, salt and pepper for 30 minutes. Remove chicken from marinade, pat dry. Reserve marinade.

Heat olive oil in a skillet. Brown chicken on both sides. Add grapes and the reserved marinade. Cook over high heat for 7 to 8 minutes until chicken is done. Stir in the cream cheese until sauce thickens. Serve over egg noodles.   Serves 4.

Serve with Chardonnay.

Chicken with Prawns

An unusual recipe with a wonderful Spanish sauce.

1 pound prawns (20-25 per
  pound)
1 bay leaf
¼ cup flour
1 teaspoon salt
½ teaspoon pepper
½ teaspoon cinnamon

6 chicken breasts, boneless
  and skinless
1 tablespoon butter
1 tablespoon olive oil
Salt and freshly ground black
  pepper

Peel the prawns and set aside. Put the shells in a small sauce pan with the bay leaf and cover with 5 cups water. Bring to a boil, reduce heat and cook for 15 minutes. Drain, reserving this shrimp stock. Discard the shells and bay leaf.

Put the flour, salt, pepper and cinnamon in a bowl. Dip the chicken breasts into the flour mixture, coating the breasts on both sides. Heat the butter and olive oil in a skillet. Cook the chicken until golden on both sides; remove. In the same skillet, cook the prawns half a minute on each side; remove. Set aside.

SOFRITO:
2 tablespoons olive oil
1 onion, minced
¾ pound tomatoes, peeled,
  seeded and chopped

2 tablespoons Anisette
1 cup dry white wine

Heat the olive oil in a non-reactive skillet. Cook the onions until golden. Add the tomatoes and cook until dry. Stir in the Anisette, wine and reserved shrimp stock. Cook until reduced by half.

PICADA:
1 ounce unsweetened
  chocolate, minced or grated
3 cloves garlic, peeled and
  chopped

¼ cup whole toasted almonds
1 tablespoon parsley
Pinch of fresh thyme
Pinch of fresh oregano

In a mortar, grind together the chocolate, garlic, toasted almonds, parsley, thyme and oregano. Add a little of the reduced shrimp stock and grind the mixture to a paste. Set aside.

In a large skillet (or preferably a clay casserole that can go to the table) heat the Sofrito and stir in the Picada. This creates the sauce.

Add chicken to the sauce and cook for 5 minutes. Stir in the prawns. Season to taste with salt and pepper if needed. Cook for another 5 minutes, or until the chicken and prawns are cooked through and the sauce is thickened. Serve directly from the casserole.

Serves 6.

Serve with Champagne or sparkling wine.

Tarragon Chicken Breast Chardonnay

2 tablespoons flour
Salt and pepper
4 chicken breast halves,
  boned and skinned
2 tablespoons olive oil
8 ounces fresh mushrooms,
  sliced
½ cup sliced green onions

2 tablespoons minced shallots
1 ounce oil-packed sun-dried
  tomatoes, minced
1 teaspoon dried tarragon
½ cup dry white wine
½ cup clear chicken broth
½ cup heavy cream

Mix flour and salt and pepper in shallow dish and lightly coat chicken breasts, reserving balance of flour. Place oil in sauté skillet and heat to medium temperature. Brown chicken on all sides, then cook approximately 10 more minutes.

Add mushrooms, onions, shallots, tomatoes and tarragon, and cook 2 minutes longer. Add wine and chicken broth, reserving 2 tablespoons, and heat. Then add remaining flour, mixed with the 2 tablespoons reserved chicken broth. Stir until smooth. Add cream, lower heat and simmer to desired consistency.   Serves 4.

Serve with a lightly chilled Chardonnay.

133

Roast Chicken with Pine Nut Dressing

2 tablespoons olive oil
½ cup thinly sliced green onion
½ cup pine nuts
2 cups cooked chard, veins
   removed
1 cup bread crumbs

¼ cup grated Parmesan cheese
¼ teaspoon nutmeg
1 teaspoon poultry seasoning
½ teaspoon salt
1 egg
1 roasting chicken or capon

To make the dressing, heat the olive oil over low heat. Sauté onions until transparent and sweet tasting. Add pine nuts and cook a minute or two. Drain chard, chop fine, and add to the onions. Add the bread crumbs, cheese, nutmeg, poultry seasoning, salt and egg.

Wash inside of chicken. Dry cavity and season with salt and pepper before stuffing. Stuff the cavity, saving a little for the neck opening.

Place a crust of bread at the opening of the body cavity to hold dressing in. Pull skin as close together as possible. Put skewers across and lace together, using the end of the string to tie legs in. Stuff the neck cavity and bring skin flap back and fasten. Roast on a rack at 325 degrees for 1 ½ to 2 hours.   Serves 6.

Serve with Gewürztraminer.

Tandoori-Style Roast Chicken

1 teaspoon salt
Juice of 1 lemon
2 minced garlic cloves
2 tablespoons minced fresh
  ginger
1 teaspoon ground cumin
  seeds
1 teaspoon ground cardamom
  seeds

2 teaspoons curry powder
1 teaspoon paprika
½ cup plain yogurt
1 roasting chicken (4 pounds)
1 teaspoon black pepper
2 teaspoons salt
1 tablespoon olive oil
½ cup lemon juice

Mix together in a small bowl the salt, lemon juice, garlic, ginger, cumin, cardamom, curry, paprika and yogurt. Set this herb mixture aside. Preheat oven to 400 degrees.

Remove giblets from chicken, rinse, and scatter over the bottom of a roasting pan. Rinse chicken thoroughly inside and out, and pat dry. Mix pepper and salt and rub into the walls of the interior cavity. Run your fingers under the skin of the breast and legs, separating it gently from the meat underneath.

Distribute as evenly as possible the herb mixture between the skin and meat, then rub the olive oil over the skin of the chicken.

Place the chicken, breast-side down, on top of the giblets and roast for 30 minutes, basting after 15 minutes with the lemon juice.

Reduce heat to 375 degrees, turn the chicken breast-side up, baste once more, then roast 15 minutes longer, or until the skin is a golden brown and a thermometer inserted into the thickest part of the thigh registers between 170 and 175 degrees. Let rest 10 minutes before carving.   Serves 2 to 4.

Serve with a Zinfandel.

Mushroom-Pepper Chicken

2 ½ pounds chicken, cut into
   serving pieces
8 sliced fresh mushrooms
1 medium onion, minced
1 tablespoon paprika
1 clove garlic, minced
1 teaspoon crushed marjoram
   leaves
¼ teaspoon salt

⅛ teaspoon ground black
   pepper
¾ cup white wine
1 teaspoon cornstarch
⅔ cup plain low-fat yogurt (at
   room temperature)
1 tablespoon minced fresh
   parsley

Remove skin from chicken pieces. In a large heavy skillet, brown chicken on all sides, adding a few drops of water to start chicken browning. Add mushrooms, onion, paprika, garlic, marjoram, salt, black pepper and wine. Simmer covered until chicken juices run clear when pierced with a sharp knife, about 35 minutes. Remove chicken, keeping warm.

Blend cornstarch with 2 tablespoons water; stir into skillet. Cook and stir until thickened, about 2 minutes. Stir yogurt with a fork until smooth. Stir into liquid in skillet. Return chicken to skillet. Cook over low heat until hot.

Serve chicken with rice or egg noodles, topped with mushroom sauce and sprinkled with parsley.   Serves 4.

Serve with Sauvignon Blanc.

136

Grilled Chicken Breast
with Black Bean and Roasted Corn Salsa

8 boneless, skinless chicken
  breast halves
¾ cup olive oil
4 ears of corn
1 ½ cups dried black beans
  (soaked overnight in water)
2 garlic cloves, chopped
¼ cup finely chopped red
  onion
½ cup finely chopped red bell
  pepper

½ teaspoon ground coriander
1 ½ tablespoons red vinegar
½ tablespoon balsamic
  vinegar
½ tablespoon fresh lime juice
¼ cup chopped Italian parsley
¼ cup chopped cilantro
1 teaspoon oregano
Salt and freshly ground pepper

Marinate the chicken breasts in 8 tablespoons of the olive oil and the stems from the fresh herbs for 8 hours.

Husk the corn, and lightly coat with a little of the olive oil. Place on a baking sheet and roast at 350 degrees for about 40 minutes or until golden brown. Cool and then remove kernels, scraping the cobs and saving any liquid along with the kernels.

Drain the beans and put into a saucepan with 1 teaspoon salt, cover with water and cook over medium heat until tender. Drain.

Cook the garlic and red onions slowly over low heat in the remaining 4 tablespoons of olive oil. Add the peppers and coriander. Cook for 2 more minutes. Stir in the beans and corn. Add vinegars and lime juice. Heat to a simmer (if more liquid is needed add water). Simmer for 5 minutes. Remove from heat and mix in the parsley, cilantro and oregano. Season with salt and freshly ground pepper.

Remove the chicken from the marinade, season with salt and freshly ground pepper. Grill both sides until done, about 5 minutes each side. Serve chicken breasts on salsa and garnish with cilantro sprigs.   Serves 8.

Serve with Sauvignon Blanc.

Chicken Curry

1 medium-size chicken, 3 ½ to 4 pounds	1 teaspoon chili powder
2 medium red peppers, chopped	½ teaspoon saffron powder
1 large onion, chopped	1 tablespoon vinegar
2 cloves garlic, crushed	Salt
1 ½ cups chicken broth	1 stick cinnamon
2 teaspoons curry powder	1 piece ginger, about 1 ½ inches
	1 cup milk

Cut chicken into serving pieces and put in large pan. Add peppers, onions and garlic to the chicken in pan. Mix chicken broth with curry powder, chili powder, saffron, vinegar and salt to taste. Add to chicken with the cinnamon stick and ginger.

Simmer until half done. Then add the milk. Continue simmering. When done, remove chicken to plate and strain broth. Remove skin and bones from chicken and break or cut into large pieces. Thicken the broth with flour. Return the chicken to broth.

Serve with white rice and small bowls of crisp chopped bacon, chopped hard boiled eggs, coconut, chopped peanuts and chutney.
Serves 4 to 6.

Serve with Johannisberg Riesling.

Chicken Scallops with Tomato, Oakleaf Lettuce and Fresh Basil

2 whole chicken breasts, split, skinned and boned
2 eggs
1 cup bread crumbs
1 tablespoon minced fresh rosemary
1 tablespoon minced fresh sage
1 tablespoon minced fresh parsley
Freshly ground pepper

Olive oil for frying
Salt
6 ripe fresh tomatoes, cut into small chunks
1 ½ cups oak leaf lettuce
1 tablespoon coarsely chopped fresh basil
2 tablespoons extra virgin olive oil
A splash of balsamic vinegar
Lemon wedges

Gently pound chicken breasts to flatten them. Lightly beat eggs in bowl. On a plate, combine bread crumbs with rosemary, sage and parsley, and season with pepper. Dip chicken breasts into egg wash, then coat both sides with bread crumb mixture. Shake off excess.

Meanwhile, heat frying pan, adding your olive oil to sauté each chicken breast, about 4 to 5 minutes on each side. Salt chicken breasts once each side has been fried. Transfer to paper towels and let drain.

Combine tomatoes, lettuce and basil with olive oil and a splash of vinegar. Season with salt and pepper.

Arrange the chicken breasts on a platter and spoon salad mixture on side. Garnish with lemon wedges.   Serves 4.

Serve with a Chardonnay.

Barbecued Happy Duck

2 ducks (5 pounds each)
6 ounces plum jam
1 cup Pinot Noir
½ cup rice wine vinegar
¼ cup soy sauce

2-inch square of ginger
4 tablespoons chopped basil
4 cloves garlic, peeled
½ onion, chopped
1 jalapeño pepper, seeded

Prick duck all over with a fork. Place it in a steamer with an inch of water. Simmer for 50 to 60 minutes. Remove and cool duck. (This can be done the day before the barbecue.) This will remove some of the fat.

Cut duck into serving-size pieces.

In a food processor, combine the jam, wine, vinegar, soy sauce, ginger, basil, garlic, onion and jalapeño. Purée. Marinate the duck pieces in this purée for 1 hour.

Barbecue duck by placing a drip pan in the center of the barbecue and place hot coals around it. Place the duck in the center over the drip pan and put the lid on the barbecue. Cook until the skin is brown and duck is done.   Serves 8.

This dish is a wonderful accompaniment to a Pinot Noir.

Turkey Picadillo

1 pound ground turkey
½ cup chopped onion
¼ cup chopped red bell
  pepper
2 cloves garlic, minced
1 tablespoon oil
1 teaspoon sugar
½ teaspoon ground cinnamon
½ teaspoon ground cumin
¼ teaspoon ground cloves

1 can (14 ½ ounces) stewed
  tomatoes
1 cup chopped Granny Smith
  apples
½ cup raisins
2 tablespoons thinly sliced
  pimiento stuffed olives
Toasted sliced almonds
  (optional)

In a large skillet over medium-high heat, sauté turkey, onion, bell pepper and garlic in the oil until turkey is no longer pink.

Stir in sugar, cinnamon, cumin, cloves, tomatoes, apples, raisins and olives. Bring to a boil. Reduce heat, cover and simmer for 15 to 20 minutes.

Serve over rice. If desired, top with toasted almonds.

Makes 4 servings.

Serve with a Zinfandel or Sauvignon Blanc.

Roasted Cornish Game Hens
with Pecan-Date Stuffing

STUFFING (FOR 6 HENS):

2 cups chicken stock
½ teaspoon salt
1 tablespoon butter
¼ teaspoon ground cinnamon
¼ teaspoon ground cardamom

1 teaspoon orange rind,
  freshly grated
1 cup long grain white rice
½ cup chopped pitted dates
½ cup chopped pecans

Bring chicken stock, salt, butter, cinnamon, cardamom and orange rind to a boil. Add rice, cover and reduce heat. Simmer 20 minutes and let sit 5 minutes. Fluff with fork and stir in dates and pecans. Set aside.

6 Cornish game hens
Salt and pepper
6 tablespoons butter, softened

½ cup orange marmalade
¼ cup Gewürztraminer

Preheat oven to 350 degrees. Prepare the birds as follows.

Rinse game hens and pat dry. Salt and pepper cavity, and stuff with a generous ½ cup of stuffing mixture. Secure legs with kitchen string and place hens in a roasting pan. Brush hens with softened butter and roast for 30 minutes.

Melt orange marmalade with the wine and reduce slightly. Raise oven temperature to 400 degrees. Baste hens with marmalade mixture and continue roasting an additional 20 or 30 minutes, or until juices run clear and hens are browned. Baste occasionally with the marmalade mixture. If the hens start to darken too much, cover with aluminum foil and continue baking.   Serves 6.

Serve with a Gewürztraminer.

Grilled Cornish Game Hen Salad with Orange-Mint Dressing

2 Cornish game hens, halved
  and flattened
¾ pound mixed salad greens
20 cherry tomatoes, halved

2 medium oranges, peeled
  and sectioned
Mint sprigs

MARINADE:
¼ cup white wine vinegar
2 tablespoons olive oil
¼ cup Chardonnay
¼ cup fresh orange juice
¼ cup chopped onion

4 tablespoons chopped fresh
  mint
½ teaspoon crushed white
  peppercorns
Pinch of salt

Combine and mix marinade thoroughly. Cover hens with marinade and refrigerate for at least 2 hours.

VINAIGRETTE:
4 tablespoons chopped fresh
  mint
1 tablespoon chopped shallots
2 tablespoons white wine
  vinegar
6 tablespoons orange juice

1 teaspoon honey
¼ cup plain low-fat yogurt
1 tablespoon walnut oil
Salt, pepper and pinch of
  ground cloves to taste

Combine ingredients and mix vinaigrette thoroughly. Refrigerate.

Remove hens from marinade and pat dry. Grill hens, skin side down, for 8 to 10 minutes. Turn and continue to grill other side for an additional 10 minutes, or until hens are done. (Or, broil under a broiler for 10 minutes per side.)

Divide greens evenly on plates. Top with grilled, halved game hens and garnish with tomatoes, orange sections and mint sprigs. Drizzle with the vinaigrette.   Serves 4 as an entrée.

Recommended wine: Chardonnay.

Lavender Roasted Cornish Hens

4 Cornish hens (1 pound
   each)
4 teaspoon dried lavender,
   coarsely crushed
1 teaspoon thyme
1 teaspoon basil

4 lemon slices
1 lemon, juiced
4 tablespoons butter
Salt
½ teaspoon lemon pepper

Preheat oven to 450 degrees. Remove giblets from the hens and rinse inside and out. Pat dry.

Mix lavender, thyme and basil together in a small bowl. Rub herb mixture into the cavity of the hens. Put a lemon slice in each bird. Tie legs of each together with string. Arrange birds in a large roasting pan, without crowding them. Pour lemon juice over hens. Rub butter on hens and season with salt and pepper. Roast for 45 to 50 minutes, until hens are done.   Serves 4.

Serve with rice, asparagus and a Pinot Blanc.

Yogurt Mustard Chicken

1 teaspoon prepared Dijon
   mustard
1 cup plain yogurt
½ teaspoon black pepper
1 teaspoon thyme

1 teaspoon marjoram
4 skinless boneless chicken
   breasts
½ cup milk

Preheat oven to 400 degrees. Mix the yogurt, mustard and spices in a bowl. Immerse chicken in mixture and place in large enough baking dish that chicken pieces are in single layer. Pour remaining yogurt over chicken. Bake the chicken in center of oven for 45 to 50 minutes or until golden brown. Remove chicken from dish, set aside keeping warm.

Stir the milk into drippings over low heat, blending until smooth. Serve sauce with chicken breasts.   Serves 4.

Serve with egg noodles and a fruity Zinfandel.

Turkey Meatballs with Ginger Chutney

1 pound ground turkey breast
   meat
1 cup crushed cracker crumbs
1 egg, beaten
2 teaspoons curry powder
½ teaspoon black pepper

¼ teaspoon salt
2 tablespoons chopped green
   onions, including part of
   green
3 tablespoons white wine

Heat oven to 400 degrees. Mix all ingredients well. Shape into 1 ½-inch meatballs. Place slightly apart on a flat pan or cookie sheet that has been sprayed with non-stick cooking spray. Bake until browned and cooked inside, about 15 minutes. Meanwhile, prepare chutney.

GINGER CHUTNEY:

4 tart firm apples, peeled and
   coarsely chopped
4 ounces (1 stick) butter
2 tablespoons apple juice
2 tablespoons orange juice

2 tablespoons lemon juice
2 teaspoons orange zest
1-inch piece fresh ginger,
   pressed through garlic press
Salt

Over medium heat, sauté the apples in the butter. Stir frequently until they are golden outside and tender inside. Add apple, orange and lemon juices. Stir in orange zest and ginger; cook briefly to blend flavors. Add salt if necessary.

Serve meatballs hot with warm Ginger Chutney and steamed rice.
Serves 4 to 6.

Serve with Chardonnay or Sauvignon Blanc.

Seafood

THE HERBS & SPICES COOKBOOK

Hazelnut Crusted Salmon with Spicy Peach Sauce

1 cup ground, roasted
  hazelnuts
2 cups cracker crumbs
½ teaspoon thyme
½ teaspoon oregano
1 teaspoon cayenne pepper

1 tablespoon olive oil
4 salmon fillets (7 to 9 ounces
  each)
2 tablespoons butter
Spicy Peach Sauce (recipe
  follows)

Preheat oven to 350 degrees. Mix the ground nuts, cracker crumbs, thyme, oregano and cayenne. Oil the salmon and "bread" it with the nut-herb mixture. Brown the salmon slightly in the butter in an oven-proof frying pan.

Transfer frying pan to a 350 degree oven. Finish cooking for 8 to 10 minutes. Serve on Spicy Peach Sauce.　　　Makes 4 servings.

Spicy Peach Sauce
1 tablespoon olive oil
½ cup chopped sweet onion
4 peaches, peeled and cubed
½ cup light brown sugar

2 tablespoons raspberry
  vinegar
1 teaspoon chili powder
Salt and pepper

Heat oil in a pan, and sauté onions until they are soft, but not brown. Add peaches, sugar, vinegar and chili powder. Cook for 10 to 15 minutes. Season to taste with salt and pepper.

Serve with a Chardonnay.

Angel-Hair Pasta Sautéed
and Cooked in Fish Stock with Lobster

8 cups fish stock
2 live lobsters (1 ½ to 2
   pounds each)
3 tablespoons olive oil
4 large garlic cloves, chopped
1 ½ pounds unpeeled
   tomatoes, puréed

½ teaspoon saffron threads
½ teaspoon salt
½ pound dried angel hair
   pasta, or coiled fedelini or
   capellini pasta noodles
1 lemon cut into 6 wedges, for
   garnish

In a narrow flameproof casserole or a stock pot, bring fish stock to a boil with 4 cups water. Drop in 1 lobster (it will turn pink). As soon as it stops moving, after a minute or two, remove lobster from pot and set it aside. Bring water back to a rapid boil before dropping in the next lobster. Reserve cooking water.

Separate lobster bodies from tails; grasp body in one hand and tail in the other, twist tail and pull; it will come free easily. Reserve any juices that ooze out. Pull out claws.

Bring lobster water to a boil again and add lobster bodies; simmer for 30 minutes, covered. Meanwhile, cut each tail, with its shell, crosswise into 3 pieces. Break claws (or remove meat from claws and discard shells, if preferred). Set aside.

Meanwhile, in a wide 2-quart saucepan, heat 1 tablespoon of the olive oil and add garlic. Cook until soft and add tomatoes; cook over medium-high heat for 3 minutes. Strain lobster water and juices into saucepan, bring to a boil, and reduce sauce to exactly 4 cups. Add saffron threads and salt; cover and set aside.

Heat remaining 2 tablespoons of the olive oil in a wide flameproof clay casserole or skillet. Add pasta, breaking it up with your hands in about 3-inch pieces as you add it. Over medium heat, stir pasta with a wooden spatula for 10 to 15 minutes, until it is golden brown (the more color the pasta acquires, the more flavor it will give to this dish; but be careful not to burn it).

Bring tomato sauce mixture to a boil and pour into casserole with noodles. Stir in lobster claws (or meat), together with tail sections. Cook over medium heat, stirring all the time, until the liquid is absorbed by the pasta. Cooking time will vary according to the size and material of casserole, but it will probably be 10 to 15 minutes.

Serve with lemon wedges.   Serves 6.

Wine recommendation: Chardonnay.

Linguini with Shrimp and Pesto

1 pound linguini pasta
½ pound sliced mushrooms
  (mix any varieties)
1 tablespoon olive oil
¼ cup chopped green onions
Juice of one lemon
½ cup white wine

1 tablespoon Worcestershire
1 pound cleaned raw shrimp
½ cup chopped parsley
1 tomato, seeded and diced
4 ounces crumbled feta
  cheese

Cook pasta according to package directions. Put aside, keeping warm. Sauté sliced mushrooms in olive oil until tender. Add chopped green onions, lemon juice, wine and Worcestershire, then bring to a boil. Add shrimp and reduce heat to simmer, covered, until shrimp are done (uniformly pink in color). While shrimp are cooking, prepare pesto.

PESTO:
2-3 cloves fresh garlic
½ cup grated Parmesan cheese
2 cups fresh basil leaves

½ cup olive oil
½ cup low-fat sour cream

Purée ingredients for pesto in blender. Set aside.

Remove shrimp from heat and add the pesto. Stir until ingredients are thoroughly blended. Pour over drained hot linguini and toss until linguini and shrimp mixture are mixed. Then add parsley, tomato and feta cheese. Toss lightly again before serving.   Serves 6.

Recommended wine: Zinfandel.

Sea-Bass Baked with Fennel

2 large tomatoes, peeled and diced	1 cup chopped celery and celery leaves
2 Spanish onions, cut into rings	½ teaspoon toasted fennel seed
1 cup dry white wine	1 bay leaf
1 cup water	Salt and freshly ground pepper to taste
Juice of ½ lemon	
4 pounds bass fillets	4 tablespoons butter

Preheat oven to 350 degrees. On the bottom of a stove-to-oven baking dish (big enough to hold long fillets), lay tomatoes and onion rings. Add wine, water and lemon juice and cook on stove until tomatoes and onions start to soften. Remove from stove and let cool briefly.

Lay the fillets in the baking dish, and add celery, fennel and bay leaf. Sprinkle with salt and pepper, and dot with butter.

Cover baking dish and bake in a 350 degree oven for 20 minutes. Remove cover, raise oven heat to 400 degrees and cook for 5 more minutes.

With a slotted spatula, lift fish onto warmed serving platter. With a wooden spoon, force cooking liquid through a sieve into a bowl. Discard pulp. Season sauce to taste, and pour this fennel-tomato sauce over the fish. Garnish with fresh parsley.

Serve with boiled small red potatoes that have been tossed in butter and sprinkled with minced parsley. Serves 4.

Serve with a dry white wine.

Medallions of Salmon with Pine Nut Herb Crust

1 center cut skinless fillet of
   salmon (8 ounces)
Salt and pepper
2 ounces pine nuts
2 tablespoons finely chopped
   shallots
5 ounces butter, melted

3 ounces fine bread crumbs
1 tablespoon finely chopped
   chives
1 tablespoon finely chopped
   tarragon
1 tablespoon finely chopped
   thyme

Remove all small bones from the salmon fillet. Remove the grey area on the underside of the fillet. Place the salmon between two pieces of plastic wrap and lightly pound with flat side of a large knife until salmon fillet is an even thickness of approximately ½ to ¾ of an inch. Season with salt and pepper.

Roll salmon up in a sausage shape and wrap in a piece of plastic wrap, tying both ends tightly. Steam wrapped salmon for about 3 minutes until it holds its shape. Cool before unwrapping. Set aside.

Toast pine nuts in a 350 degree oven. Chop them finely in a food processor. Sauté chopped shallots in melted butter for about 1 minute and add bread crumbs, pine nuts and chopped herbs. Season with salt and pepper, if necessary. Let cool.

Cut salmon roll in half. The center should be raw. Cut a small piece off each end of the salmon so it can stand upright. Press a small mound of pine nut mixture on top of each salmon medallion. Place medallion on an oiled sheet pan in a 400 degree oven for approximately 4 minutes. Serve with beurre blanc sauce.

Serves 2.

Serve with Chardonnay.

Cilantro Cured Salmon

1 whole tail section of fresh
  salmon, about 2 pounds
3 tablespoons coarse salt
2 tablespoons sugar
2 tablespoons ground pasilla
  (or other mild) chile pepper

2 bunches fresh cilantro
2 medium or 1 large jicama
4 tablespoons lime juice
1 cup plain yogurt, low-fat or
  nonfat (optional)

Have your fishmonger scale and butterfly salmon, removing all bones. When finished, salmon should open like a book, with skin side out.

Mix salt, sugar and pasilla pepper together, and rub over all surfaces of the fish.

Wash and coarsely chop one bunch of cilantro. Make a bed of ⅓ of the cilantro on a glass or ceramic dish that will hold the salmon.

Place salmon, skin side down, on the cilantro and distribute ⅓ on flesh. Fold fish back together and cover top with remaining cilantro. Cover securely with plastic wrap and weight the fish with a brick or an iron frying pan. Refrigerate for 48 to 72 hours, turning fish occasionally.

Peel jicama and cut in thin slices, about 1/8-inch thick. Cut into decorative shapes with a cookie cutter, if desired. Place in a shallow bowl and cover with lime juice. Wipe marinade off salmon and cut on the bias into thin slices*, detaching the slices from the skin as you go. Place pieces of salmon on jicama slices and top with fresh cilantro leaves. Or, mix ⅓ cup minced cilantro leaves with yogurt and place a small spoonful on each plate.

  Serves 6 as first course, or 18 to 20 as an appetizer.

Serve with Sauvignon Blanc.

For appetizer, cut into 1-inch square pieces.

Oven-Roasted Salmon
with an Orange and Dill Beurre Blanc

4 salmon fillets (5 ounces each) with the skin removed
Salt and pepper
1 cup plus 3 tablespoons sweet unsalted butter
1 cup sparkling wine

2 medium shallots, chopped
⅓ cup whipping cream
Zest of 1 orange
¼ cup chopped fresh dill
3 tablespoons light oil (olive or safflower)

Preheat oven to 450 degrees.

Check salmon fillets for small bones. Season fish with salt and pepper. Refrigerate. Cut 1 cup of the butter into small pieces and refrigerate.

To prepare the beurre blanc sauce, place wine and shallots in a medium sauce pan. Cook on medium low for 15 minutes, until wine mixture is reduced. Add cream and continue cooking for 10 minutes. Watch closely, stirring, so that it won't boil over. Remove from heat and pour into blender. Add the cup of cold butter pieces to the wine. Blend slowly with low power and continue blending until mixture is smooth. Pour mixture into top of a double boiler on low heat. Add orange zest, chopped dill and salt and pepper to taste. Keep warm over low heat.

Cook the salmon in a large, hot skillet in the remaining 3 tablespoons butter and the oil. Cook for 1 ½ minutes on each side until browned. Place in oven for 5 more minutes to finish cooking.

Serve salmon topped with beurre blanc sauce. Garnish with orange slices and a sprig of dill. Accompany with wilted spinach and creamy mashed potatoes.
                                                                Serves 4.

Serve with sparkling wine.

Herb Baked Salmon with
Lobster Lemon Thyme Cream Sauce

4 salmon fillets (6 ounces each)
¼ cup dry white wine
1 tablespoon chopped fresh thyme
1 tablespoon chopped fresh cilantro

1 tablespoon chopped fresh basil
1 tablespoon chopped fresh lemon balm*
Butter

Place salmon on greased pan. Splash with wine and dust with thyme, cilantro, basil and lemon balm. Dot with small amount of butter. Bake at 375 degrees for 10 to 15 minutes. Check while cooking. Fish should not be overcooked.

LOBSTER LEMON THYME CREAM SAUCE:
½ cup dry white wine
½ cup fish stock
1 teaspoon chopped lemon thyme
4 teaspoons lemon juice

1 chopped shallot
½ cup cream
½ pound fresh lobster meat
Salt and pepper

Combine wine, stock, lemon thyme, lemon juice and shallot in a sauce pan. Bring to a boil and reduce liquid by ⅓. Add cream and lobster meat, simmering until lobster is warm and sauce is correct consistency. Season with salt and pepper to taste.

Serve salmon topped with sauce and a sprig of fresh lemon thyme.
Serves 4.

Serve with Chardonnay.

Lemon balm has lemon scented mint-like leaves, and can be found in gourmet grocery and specialty stores.

Peppered Salmon with Lavender

2 tablespoons whole black
    peppercorns
4 tablespoons dried lavender*
3 pounds fresh salmon, cut in
    1-inch slices
2 tablespoons olive oil

2 tablespoons butter
3 tablespoons minced shallots
1 cup chicken stock
1 cup Cabernet Sauvignon
4 tablespoons softened butter

Crush peppercorns with a pestle or process with steel blade in a food processor. Mix crushed peppercorns with lavender and press into both sides of the salmon slices. Cover and let stand at least ½ hour, or up to 3 hours for maximum pepper flavor.

In a sauté pan, sear over high heat in the oil and butter for 3 to 4 minutes on each side. (This is a dish that can be served rare.) Check for desired doneness by piercing with the point of a small, sharp knife.

Hold fish in a warm oven while making the sauce. Add shallots to sauté pan and cook about 1 minute. Deglaze the pan with the stock, then add the Cabernet and cook rapidly until reduced by half. Remove pan from heat and stir in butter.

Pour sauce over salmon and serve immediately.   Serves 6.

Suggested wine: Cabernet Sauvignon.

Dried lavender is available in most supermarkets in the spice section, and in many health food stores.

Scallop Sauté with Leek and Allspice

3 tablespoons melted butter
1 ½ pounds scallops
1 white leek, cut in rings and
   separated
1 cup Sauvignon Blanc or
   other dry white wine

½ teaspoon allspice
¼ teaspoon salt
¼ teaspoon cayenne pepper
2 tablespoons cold butter, cut
   in small pieces

Place the melted butter in a pan large enough to hold all your scallops in a single layer. Add the scallops and leeks simultaneously, tossing or stirring gently over medium heat. Be careful, leeks burn more readily than other onions.

When the scallops are opaque, but still spring back a little to the touch, pour in the wine and add the seasonings. When the wine simmers, remove the scallops with a slotted spoon to a heated serving dish or bed of rice.

Raise the heat to reduce the wine and scallop juices to a thick syrup. Remove the pan from the heat and swirl in the cold butter bit by bit, returning to low heat briefly as required. The butter will blend most easily if taken out of the refrigerator a half hour before it is needed. When all the butter has been incorporated, pour this sauce over the scallops.   Serves 4.

Serve with Sauvignon Blanc.

Sautéed Medallions of Tuna
with Papaya Salsa and Cilantro Pesto

1 cup chopped cilantro
3 cloves garlic, chopped
5 tablespoons olive oil
2 tablespoons finely chopped
  ginger
2 tablespoons chopped
  scallions
2 tablespoons toasted pine
  nuts

½ teaspoon salt
1 cup diced ripe papaya
1 tablespoon chopped mint
  leaves
2 tablespoons olive oil
12 medallions of tuna fillets (1
  ½ ounces each)
Salt and white pepper

First make the pesto by combining the cilantro, garlic, olive oil, ginger, scallions, nuts and salt in a food processor. Blend until well mixed.

For the salsa, mix together the diced papaya and mint. Set aside.

Heat olive oil in a skillet. Season tuna with salt and white pepper. Sauté on both sides for 2 to 3 minutes on each side, until cooked through.

Serve on hot plates, 2 medallions per plate. Top with cilantro pesto. Spoon the salsa on the side of the plate. Serve immediately.

Serves 6.

Suggested wine: Chardonnay or Johannisberg Riesling.

Seafood and Kielbasa Sausage Gumbo

½ cup vegetable oil
¼ cup margarine
¾ cup flour
2 cups chopped onions
2 cups chopped red or yellow
  bell peppers
1 ½ cups chopped celery
3 or 4 bay leaves
¾ teaspoon salt
¾ teaspoon cayenne pepper
½ teaspoon white pepper
¼ teaspoon black pepper
¼ teaspoon thyme

¼ teaspoon oregano
1 tablespoon crushed garlic
6 cups seafood stock or clam
  juice
1 pound kielbasa sausage
¾ pound fresh halibut fillet (cut
  into ½-inch pieces)
1 pound medium shrimp
¾ pound fresh crabmeat
1 can (15 ounces) cut okra
1 cup dry white wine
8 to 10 cups hot cooked rice

Heat oil and margarine in large skillet over high heat until it smokes. Gradually whisk in flour and, whisking continuously, make a roux with dark brown consistency. Do not burn roux.

Immediately add half the onions, peppers and celery. Stir 2 minutes, add remaining onions, peppers and celery. Add bay leaves, salt, cayenne pepper, white pepper, black pepper, thyme, oregano and garlic. Cook 3 to 4 minutes.

In a 5-quart pot, add seafood stock and bring to a boil. Add roux mixture a spoonful at a time, stirring until dissolved.

Add kielbasa sausage and continue boiling 15 minutes, stirring occasionally. Reduce heat and simmer 10 minutes more. Return to boil, add halibut, shrimp, crabmeat, okra and wine. Remove from heat. Let stand 10 minutes to poach seafood. Skim any oil from surface. Serve immediately.

To serve, mound 1 cup cooked rice in middle of bowl and spoon a cup of gumbo over top.   Serves 8 to 10.

Serve with Chardonnay.

California Fish Soup

½ teaspoon saffron threads
3 tablespoons olive oil
3 cloves garlic, minced
1 medium onion, peeled and
   diced
1 leek, washed and sliced
   (white, with part of
   green)
½ cup diced celery
½ teaspoon paprika
3 medium potatoes, peeled
   and cubed
3 medium tomatoes, peeled
   and chopped
1 bay leaf

2-3 sprigs fresh thyme, or 1
   teaspoon dried
3 sprigs parsley
2 strips fresh orange peel (½
   inch wide by 2 inches long)
5 cups water
1 cup dry white wine
Sea salt and freshly ground
   black pepper
2 ½ pounds assorted boned
   fresh white fish, such as
   halibut, cod, bass, red
   snapper or sole, cut into 2-
   inch pieces
Cayenne pepper

Place the saffron and a pinch of salt in a metal kitchen spoon. Hold over heat for a few seconds to get warm and, with a teaspoon, crush thread to a powder. Set aside.

Heat olive oil in a large saucepan. Add garlic, onion, leek, celery and paprika. Cook gently for 2 to 3 minutes, while stirring, until onion is transparent. Add potatoes, tomatoes, bay leaf, thyme, parsley and orange peel. Cover and gently cook for 5 minutes, stirring occasionally.

Add the prepared saffron, water, wine, a dash of sea salt and freshly ground pepper. Cover and simmer for 20 to 25 minutes. Add the fish, adding a little more water or wine if necessary.

Cover and cook at a gentle simmer for 10 to 15 minutes until fish is just cooked through (depending on size of fish pieces). Do not overcook. Check seasonings, adding a dash of cayenne pepper if desired.
                                                        Serves 6.

Serve with French Bread and a Chardonnay.

Shanghai Lobster Risotto with
Spicy Ginger and Julienne of Green Onions

1 piece (1 inch) fresh ginger
2 cloves garlic, minced
¾ cup plum wine or Port
2 tablespoons rice wine
  vinegar
2 tablespoons peanut oil
1 lobster (2 pounds) split
  lengthwise
2 tablespoons unsalted butter
4 scallions, cut into 3/8-inch
  slices
1-2 teaspoons curry powder

¼ cup dry white wine
½ cup fish stock
½ teaspoon dried hot chili
  flakes
1 tablespoon balsamic vinegar
½ cup heavy cream
Salt
Freshly ground pepper
1 teaspoon minced candied
  ginger
Risotto (recipe follows)

Preheat oven to 500 degrees. Peel the ginger, reserving the peels, and cut it into fine julienne strips. Cut the peels into coarse julienne strips and set aside.

In a small saucepan, cook the ginger and garlic with ½ cup of the plum wine and the rice wine vinegar until 1 tablespoon of liquid remains. Remove from the heat and reserve.

Place a heavy 12-inch skillet over high heat until it is very hot. Add the oil and heat it almost to the smoking point. Carefully add the lobster halves, meat side down. Cook 3 minutes. Turn the lobster over and add 1 tablespoon of the butter. Continue to sauté until the lobster shells are getting red and the butter is nutty red. Transfer the lobster to the oven for about 10 minutes, or until the lobster is just cooked. Remove from the oven, remove the lobster from the skillet and keep warm.

Add the scallions, ginger peels and curry powder to the skillet. (Be careful the handle might be hot.) Sauté the mixture lightly for 10 to 15 minutes, then whisk in the remaining plum wine and the white wine, fish stock, chili flakes and the vinegar. Reduce the liquid to ½ cup. Add the cream and reduce it by half. Add any liquid from the julienne of ginger, then whisk in the remaining tablespoon butter. Season the sauce to taste with salt and pepper.

Crack the lobster claws with the back of a large chef's knife.

Arrange the lobster halves on a warm oval platter, meat side up. Strain the sauce over the lobster, then sprinkle with candied ginger on top. Serve with Risotto.

Serves 2.

RISOTTO:
1 cup arborio rice
4 cups fish stock

Sauté rice in remaining 1 tablespoon butter to coat well. Add 2 cups fish stock, bring to a boil. Then, turn to low heat to simmer, stirring and adding more stock as it is absorbed by the rice. Cook until tender, about 40 to 45 minutes.

Serve with Champagne or other sparkling wine.

Sea Bass Fillets Baked in Herbed-Wine

½ cup Chardonnay
½ cup clam juice
4 sea bass fillets (6 ounces each)
Juice of 1 lemon

Salt and pepper
1 tablespoon chopped fresh marjoram
1 tablespoon chopped fresh basil

Preheat oven to 400 degrees. Heat the wine and clam juice in a small pan over medium high heat until the liquid comes to a boil.

Carefully place the sea bass fillets in a lightly oiled glass baking dish. Sprinkle the lemon juice over the fish. Season with salt and pepper. Sprinkle the marjoram and basil over each fillet. Then, pour wine mixture around fish.

Cover the baking dish with foil. Bake for 5 to 7 minutes, or until the centers of the fillets are sufficiently cooked. Serve immediately.

Serves 4.

Serve with Chardonnay.

Vegetables

THE HERBS & SPICES COOKBOOK

Potato and Butternut Squash Gratin
with Caramelized Onions and Fresh Thyme

½ cup plus 2 tablespoons
  unsalted butter
4 cloves garlic, finely minced
  or pressed
4 large onions, peeled and cut
  into ½-inch slices
4 large white-skinned potatoes
1 small butternut squash,
  peeled and seeded

Salt and freshly ground pepper
2 tablespoons chopped fresh
  thyme
3 tablespoons extra virgin
  olive oil
¾ cup toasted bread crumbs,
  seasoned with olive oil, garlic
  and salt and pepper

Butter a 9 × 13-inch baking dish with 2 tablespoons of the butter. Sprinkle 1 clove of the minced garlic over the bottom of the pan and set it aside. Preheat oven to 375 degrees.

Caramelize the onions by sautéing the onions in the remaining ½ cup butter over medium heat until translucent. Continue to stir the onions as they brown. The onions are done when they are quite brown for the best true caramel flavor.

While the onions are caramelizing, slice both the potatoes and the squash into very thin slices. In the prepared baking dish arrange a layer of half the potatoes in bottom of dish. Sprinkle with a little salt and pepper. Arrange ½ of the squash slices on top of the potatoes. Sprinkle with 1 clove of the minced garlic, salt, pepper and 1 tablespoon of thyme.

Spread caramelized onions over squash. Top with the rest of the squash, garlic, salt, pepper and thyme. Layer balance of potatoes on top. Drizzle olive oil on top.

Cover with foil and bake at 375 degrees for one hour. Remove foil, sprinkle seasoned bread crumbs on top of the gratin and bake another 6 to 7 minutes. Remove from oven, cut into squares, and serve while hot.   Makes 10 to 12 side dish servings.

Vegetables

Garlic Mashed Potatoes

2 pounds potatoes, peeled
  and quartered
4 large cloves garlic, peeled
¼ cup grated Parmesan
  cheese
½ cup milk

¼ cup low-fat sour cream
½ teaspoon salt
¼ teaspoon black pepper
¼ cup chopped fresh parsley

Boil potatoes and garlic in a large saucepan in enough water to cover potatoes. Cook until tender, about 25 to 30 minutes.

Drain potatoes and garlic into a colander; then return them to the saucepan. Add cheese, milk, sour cream, salt and pepper. Mash or beat with electric mixer until blended. Add parsley and mix until creamy.   Serves 6.

Nutmeg-Onion Potato Bake

4 medium potatoes, cut in
  pieces
2 large onions, chopped
1 cup water
1 cup milk
3 tablespoons butter
Salt and pepper

¼ teaspoon nutmeg
2 tablespoons fresh chopped
  parsley
¼ cup grated Parmesan
  cheese
Dash of cinnamon

Simmer potatoes, onions, milk and water in covered pan until tender.

Drain potatoes, reserving liquid. Mash potatoes with 2 tablespoons of the butter, salt and pepper, and nutmeg. Add reserved liquid as needed to mash. If there is not enough liquid, use additional milk. Mix in parsley. Place potatoes in a buttered casserole. Sprinkle cheese on top. Dot with remaining 1 tablespoon butter. Sprinkle with cinnamon. Bake for 20 minutes, or until topping has browned.
                                    Serves 4 to 6.

Lavender Roasted Red Potatoes

1 teaspoon dried lavender
¼ teaspoon salt
¼ teaspoon cracked black
  pepper
1 pound small new red
  potatoes, halved

½ pound small white pearl
  onions, peeled
2 tablespoons olive oil

Heat oven to 400 degrees. In a small bowl, combine lavender, salt and pepper.

In a large bowl, toss potatoes and onions in the olive oil along with the lavender mixture. Place vegetables on a baking sheet and roast for 40 to 45 minutes, or until vegetables are tender and browned. Stir occasionally and loosen from baking sheet with a spatula.

Serve with your favorite roast chicken or lamb dish.   Serves 4.

Roasted Red Potatoes with Garlic and Thyme

8-10 small red potatoes
10 cloves of garlic
¼ cup olive oil

1 tablespoon dried thyme (or 2
  tablespoons fresh)
Salt and pepper

Wash the potatoes and pat dry with a paper towel. Cut them in half and place in a glass baking dish. Peel the garlic cloves, leaving them whole, and sprinkle them among the potatoes in the pan. Pour the olive oil over the potatoes and garlic, then sprinkle with the thyme.

Bake in a 375 degree oven for about an hour, or until the potatoes are soft when tested with a fork. Season with salt and pepper to taste. An easy, flavorful way to roast potatoes.   Serves 4

Baked Sweet Potatoes with Apples

4 large sweet potatoes (3-4 pounds)

2 large tart apples, peeled and sliced

½ cup Riesling or Chenin Blanc

½ teaspoon ground cinnamon

½ teaspoon salt

⅛ teaspoon white pepper

4 tablespoons butter

Boil potatoes for 25 minutes. Cool, peel and cut into 1/8-inch slices. Layer potatoes and apple slices in a 2-quart casserole, beginning and ending with potatoes. Combine wine and seasonings. Add to casserole. Dot top with butter.

Cover tightly and bake at 350 degrees for 20 minutes. Remove cover and continue baking for another 20 minutes. Serves 4 to 6.

Spiced Roasted Garlic Cloves

2 cups peeled garlic cloves

Salt

Freshly ground pepper

2 tablespoons fresh rosemary

1 tablespoon fresh thyme

¼ teaspoon chili pepper flakes

½ to ¾ cup olive oil

In a glass, oven-proof baking dish (12 × 14 inches) scatter garlic cloves, salt and pepper, rosemary, thyme and chili pepper flakes. Drizzle olive oil over all. Cover pan with aluminum foil. Bake in 350 degree oven for 1 hour or until cloves are nicely browned and glazed.

You can use these several ways. Use them as is, spread them on bread, or purée to use in place of butter. They make a nice addition to soups and dressings, and will keep very well if refrigerated.

Onions in Chardonnay Cream

2 pounds small white onions
1 ½ cups Chardonnay
6 tablespoons butter
1 bay leaf
½ teaspoon crumbled dried
   thyme
½ teaspoon salt

¼ teaspoon white pepper
1 teaspoon grated lemon rind
2 tablespoons flour
½ cup heavy cream
2 tablespoons chopped
   parsley

Blanch onions in boiling water for 1 minute. Drain, rinse under cold running water, and peel. In skillet, combine wine, 4 tablespoons of the butter, bay leaf, thyme, salt, pepper and lemon rind. Bring to a boil. Add onions. Cover and simmer about 20 minutes, turning onions occasionally, until tender. Remove onions with slotted spoon. Boil cooking liquid until reduced to about 1 cup.

In medium saucepan, combine flour with the remaining 2 tablespoons butter and cook for 1 minute. Slowly whisk in reduced liquid and cream. Bring to a boil over medium heat, stirring constantly. Add onions, lower heat and continue cooking just until onions are heated through. Transfer to heated serving bowls. Sprinkle with chopped parsley.   Serves 8.

Mediterranean Green Beans

1 tablespoon olive oil
1 medium onion, sliced thin
1 cup chopped tomatoes
½ garlic clove, minced
1 teaspoon paprika
1 teaspoon thyme leaves

⅛ teaspoon black pepper
1 strip orange rind
1 cup water
1 pound fresh green beans,
   cut into 1 ½-inch pieces

In medium saucepan, heat oil, add onion and sauté until golden, about 1 minute. Add tomatoes, garlic, paprika, thyme, black pepper, orange rind and water. Bring to boil, reduce heat and simmer 5 minutes before adding beans. Cook, covered, until crisp tender, about 10 minutes. Remove orange rind before serving. Serves 4.

Parsley Creamed Carrots

2 tablespoons butter
3 cups sliced carrots
1 cup chopped onions
Salt and pepper
½ cup chicken broth

3 tablespoons cream cheese
½ cup milk
1 teaspoon nutmeg
2 tablespoons minced fresh
   parsley

Melt butter in a heavy saucepan. Add carrots, onions, and salt and pepper to taste. Sauté for 5 minutes until onions are transparent. Add chicken broth and cook for 15 minutes, or until carrots are tender.

Remove carrots and onions from saucepan. Set aside and keep warm.

Put cream cheese and milk in saucepan with broth. Stir and blend in cheese until sauce is smooth. Season with nutmeg. Return carrots and onions to saucepan, mixing well. Garnish with parsley.

Serves 4.

Spiced Carrots

2 cups julienned carrots
¾ cup pineapple juice
¾ teaspoon ground cinnamon

⅛ teaspoon ground nutmeg
Sprinkle of black pepper

In a saucepan, combine carrots, pineapple juice, cinnamon, nutmeg and pepper. Bring to a boil. Reduce heat to simmer. Cook, covered, about 15 minutes until carrots are crisp-tender.   Serves 4 to 6.

Spicy Broccoli

3 cups broccoli florets
2 tablespoons olive oil
1 medium onion, chopped
¼ cup chopped fresh parsley
1 teaspoon grated fresh lemon
　peel

¼ cup white wine
2 teaspoons chopped basil
¼ teaspoon dried crushed red
　pepper
½ cup grated Parmesan
　cheese

Steam broccoli until just tender, 3 to 4 minutes.

Heat olive oil in medium frying pan over medium heat. Add chopped onion and sauté until soft, about 6 minutes. Add chopped parsley, lemon peel, wine , basil and crushed red pepper. Stir while cooking, 2 minutes. Add broccoli and toss until coated. Add salt and pepper to taste. Sprinkle cheese on top.　　　　Serves 4.

Spiced Red Cabbage

1 medium head red cabbage,
　washed, cored and
　shredded
⅔ cup red wine vinegar
¼ teaspoon ground cloves
2 tablespoons sugar
1 teaspoon salt
2 tablespoons olive oil

2 medium tart apples, peeled,
　cored and sliced
½ cup chopped onion
1 bay leaf
1 cup red wine
3 cups boiling water
¼ teaspoon black pepper

Put the shredded cabbage in a large bowl. Sprinkle with vinegar, cloves, sugar and salt. Toss the cabbage to coat. Set aside.

In a large skillet or saucepan, heat olive oil. Add apples and onions. Cook for 5 to 8 minutes until apples are browned. Add the cabbage and the bay leaf. Mix throughly. Add wine and boiling water. Return to a boil, stirring often. Reduce heat, cover and simmer for 1 hour, or until cabbage is tender.

Remove bay leaf. Add pepper, and salt if needed.　　　Serves 6.

Tomato-Zucchini Bake

3 cups thinly sliced zucchini
4 fresh tomatoes, sliced
1 medium onion, sliced thin
2 tablespoons fresh chopped
  parsley
½ clove garlic, minced fine
1 ½ teaspoons chili powder

Salt and pepper to taste
¼ cup fresh white bread
  crumbs
1 tablespoon olive oil
2 tablespoons grated
  Parmesan cheese

Preheat oven to 375 degrees. In a lightly greased 6-cup casserole, layer half the zucchini, tomatoes and onion. Sprinkle with half of the parsley, garlic, chili powder, salt and pepper. Repeat layering with balance of zucchini, tomatoes and onion. Sprinkle with remaining garlic, chili powder, salt and pepper. Mix the bread crumbs with the olive oil. Top beans with bread crumbs. Sprinkle grated cheese on top.

Bake, uncovered, until vegetables are tender, about 35 to 40 minutes.
Serves 4.

Vegetable Ragout

1 cup sweet butter
1 cup sliced white onions
1 cup thinly sliced red bell
  pepper
1 cup thinly sliced yellow bell
  pepper

2 cups sliced mushrooms
1 cup sliced zucchini
2 cloves garlic, minced
2 tablespoons chopped fresh
  tarragon
Salt and pepper

Heat the butter in a large pan until very hot. Add the onions and cook until translucent. Stir in the red and yellow peppers and allow to cook 2 to 3 minutes. Add the mushrooms, zucchini, garlic and tarragon. Simmer for 15 minutes. Season with salt and pepper.
Serves 4 to 6.

Broccoli with Hazelnuts

1 onion, peeled and
   minced
½ cup chopped toasted
   hazelnuts
3 tablespoons butter

2 heads fresh broccoli
   (approximately 1 ½ pounds)
1 teaspoon finely chopped
   rosemary leaves
Salt and pepper to taste

Sauté the onion and hazelnuts in the butter until the onion is translucent.

Add the broccoli, sprinkle with rosemary. Cover and cook on low heat until the broccoli is tender. (Add a small amount of water during cooking, if necessary, to keep the vegetables from sticking to the pan.) Add salt and pepper, and stir gently.   Serves 4 to 6.

Sautéed Cucumbers

2 large cucumbers, peeled
1 medium onion, minced
2 tablespoons butter or
   margarine
2 tablespoons flour

¾ cup half-and-half
1 tablespoon dried fill weed
1 teaspoon granulated sugar
Salt to taste
Dash of white pepper

Cut peeled cucumbers in half lengthwise and scrape out seeds with a spoon. Cut cucumbers in ½-inch cubes. Sauté cucumber and onions in butter in a large, heavy pan until tender, but still firm, about 2 minutes. Sprinkle with flour and stir to blend. Add half-and-half, dill, sugar, salt and pepper.

Cook over moderate heat until thickened, stirring constantly. If serving is delayed and sauce becomes too thick, add a little more half-and-half.
                                                        Serves 4.

Mint Glazed Carrots

1 ½ pounds medium carrots
2 tablespoons butter or
  margarine
⅓ cup light brown sugar

Salt and pepper
2 teaspoons chopped fresh
  mint

Peel and cut the carrots in half lengthwise. Heat 1 inch of water to boil in a 12-inch skillet. Add carrots and return to boil. Reduce heat to low; cover and simmer for 10 to 15 minutes, until vegetables are almost tender. Drain off water.

Add butter and brown sugar to carrots. Cook over medium-high heat, gently turning carrots occasionally until sugar dissolves and carrots are glazed and golden, about 10 minutes. Stir in chopped mint. Season with salt and pepper to taste.   Makes 6 servings.

Southern Green Beans

1 pound fresh green beans,
  trimmed
Boiling water to cover
¼ pound ham, sliced ¼-inch
  thick and cut into 2-inch
  strips

½ cup finely chopped onion
⅓ cup cider vinegar
1 tablespoon sugar
1 teaspoon chopped rosemary
  leaves
Salt and pepper to taste

Put green beans in a large pot of boiling water. Cook about 6 minutes until beans are tender. Drain the beans and rinse under cold water. Pat dry and reserve.

Cook ham in a large skillet over medium heat until brown and crisp. Drain on paper towels. Pour off all but 1 tablespoon drippings.

Add the onion to the skillet; sauté for 3 to 5 minutes, or until tender. Add the ham, then the vinegar, sugar, rosemary, salt and pepper. Cook, stirring, until mixture is hot and bubbly. Add cooked beans; toss to coat. Serve hot.   Serves 4.

Desserts

THE HERBS & SPICES COOKBOOK

Cinnamon Chocolate Pecan Pie

One 9-inch pie crust

FILLING:
1 cup light corn syrup
½ cup sugar
¼ cup margarine or butter,
  melted
1 teaspoon vanilla

1 teaspoon cinnamon
3 eggs
1 cup semi-sweet chocolate
  chips
1 ½ cups pecan halves

TOPPING:
Whipped cream
½ teaspoon cinnamon

1 teaspoon powdered sugar

Prepare pie crust according to package directions, using a 9-inch pie pan. Heat oven to 325 degrees.

In a large bowl, combine corn syrup, sugar, margarine, vanilla, cinnamon and eggs, and beat well. Stir in chocolate chips and pecans. Spread evenly in pie crust. Bake at 325 degrees for 55 to 65 minutes, or until pie is a deep golden brown and filling is set. Cover edge of pie crust with strip of foil after 15 to 20 minutes of baking to prevent excessive browning. Cool completely.

Garnish pie with whipped cream to which you have added cinnamon and powdered sugar. Refrigerate.   Serves 8.

Pumpkin Ice Cream Pie

1 prepared graham cracker
  crust
1 cup canned pumpkin
½ cup brown sugar
½ teaspoon cinnamon
¼ teaspoon ground ginger

¼ teaspoon ground cloves
⅛ teaspoon ground nutmeg
1 quart vanilla ice cream
¼ cup toasted pecan halves
Whipped cream, for garnish

Bake graham cracker crust according to package directions. Set aside to cool.

Combine pumpkin, sugar, cinnamon, ginger, cloves and nutmeg in a large saucepan over medium heat, stirring constantly to blend spices and melt the sugar. Put aside and cool completely.

Put slightly softened ice cream into the cold pumpkin mixture and blend.

Spread pumpkin ice cream mixture into pie crust. Decorate top with pecan halves. Freeze pie.

Remove from freezer 20 minutes before serving. Serve with whipped cream and a sprinkle of nutmeg.   Serves 6 to 8.

Caramel Surprise Apple Pie

1 ready-prepared pie crust	½ teaspoon finely grated
4 cups sliced peeled apples	lemon peel
¼ cup brown sugar	⅔ cup brown sugar
1 teaspoon cinnamon	¼ cup cream
½ teaspoon nutmeg	4 tablespoons butter
2 tablespoons plus 2	2 teaspoons vanilla
teaspoons flour	

Preheat oven to 375 degrees. Prepare pie crust according to package directions. Place bottom crust in a 9-inch pan. Set top crust aside.

Toss the sliced apples with the ¼ cup brown sugar, cinnamon, nutmeg, 2 tablespoons of the flour and lemon peel.

Sprinkle the remaining 2 teaspoons flour over the bottom of the unbaked pie shell. Put the apple mixture in the pie shell and set aside.

To make the caramel sauce, put the remaining ⅔ cup brown sugar, cream, and butter in a saucepan. Heat, stirring constantly, until butter is melted and the sugar is completely dissolved. Add vanilla and stir until sauce is smooth.

Pour caramel sauce over apple filling. Cut a few vents in top crust, and cover pie. Seal the two crusts, crimping the edges.

Bake for 50 to 55 minutes, until the crust is lightly browned and apples are tender.

Serve with vanilla ice cream for a special treat.   Serves 6 to 8.

Ricotta Cheese-Lemon Thyme Tart
with Sweet Cornmeal Crust

CORNMEAL CRUST:
½ cup butter, at room
  temperature
¼ cup sugar
1 cup yellow cornmeal

2 eggs, at room temperature
1 teaspoon salt
1 ½ cups all-purpose flour

Beat butter and sugar until smooth. Add cornmeal, eggs, and salt, and beat until well combined. Add flour and mix until dough forms a ball. Mixture should be soft and moist. Wrap in plastic and chill for 1 hour. Roll out the crust to fit a 9-inch by 1-inch tart pan with removable bottom. Wrap and save any leftover dough in freezer. Prick with a fork several times and bake for 8 minutes at 350 degrees until just lightly brown. (Leftover dough is good for making biscuits.)

RICOTTA CHEESE-LEMON THYME FILLING:
4 tablespoons minced shallots
  or green onions
1 tablespoon butter
⅔ cup heavy cream
½ cup Fumé Blanc
½ teaspoon salt
¼ teaspoon ground white
  pepper

12 ounces fresh ricotta cheese
3 eggs
1 ½ tablespoons chopped
  fresh lemon thyme or other
  fresh herbs (chives, parsley,
  basil)

Sauté shallots in butter until soft, not brown. Add cream, wine, salt and white pepper. Reduce by one half. Cool. Add ricotta cheese, eggs and thyme, and beat until smooth. Pour into the prepared tart shell.

Bake in a 350 degree oven for 35 to 40 minutes, or until filling is just set and lightly browned. Serve warm, or at room temperature. Garnish with a sprinkling of edible flowers.　　　　Serves 6.

Recommended wine: Fumé Blanc. The crisp flavors of the wine play a perfect counterpart to the tart.

Baked Peaches with Warm Raspberry Compote

HAZELNUT MIXTURE:
1 cup ground hazelnuts
¼ cup cream cheese
1 tablespoon sour cream
½ teaspoon cinnamon
¼ teaspoon allspice
1 large egg
Sugar

RASPBERRY COMPOTE:
4 pints fresh raspberries
2 tablespoons unsalted butter
½ cup Sémillon wine
2 tablespoons sugar
1 tablespoon lemon zest

PEACHES:
3 ripe peaches
1 cup Sémillon wine

PREPARE HAZELNUT MIXTURE:
Mix the hazelnuts with the cream cheese and sour cream. Mix well. Stir in the cinnamon, allspice, and egg. Add sugar to taste. Reserve.

PREPARE RASPBERRY COMPOTE:
Sauté raspberries in butter. Add wine and sugar and bring to a boil. Add zest.

PREPARE PEACHES:
Cut peaches in half, remove pit and hollow out slightly. Fill with hazelnut mixture and bake in a 325 degree oven, covered, for 30 minutes.

TO FINISH:
Remove peaches from oven. Pour raspberry sauce onto each plate and place a peach half on top. Just before serving, drizzle with a splash of wine. Garnish with fresh mint and flowers. Serve warm.

Serves 6.

Caramel Lavender Ice Cream

6 egg yolks
⅔ cup sugar
Seeds scraped from 1 vanilla
  bean

1 cup heavy cream
2 cups milk
1 ½ teaspoons dried lavender
¾ cup honey

Cream egg yolks and sugar until thick and ribbon-like. Add the seeds from vanilla bean. Bring heavy cream, milk and lavender to boil. Very slowly, strain into the egg mixture while continuously beating.

In a heavy sauce pan, caramelize honey by heating and stirring until it becomes a golden to deep brown.

Put the milk and egg mixture back on the stove, turn heat to low, and slowly add caramelized honey, whisking continuously.

Cool in refrigerator 1 ½ to 2 hours, then freeze in ice cream maker according to manufacturer's directions.   Makes about 1 ½ quarts.

Chocolate Lavender Truffles

1 cup heavy cream
1 ½ teaspoons dried lavender
12 ounces bittersweet
  chocolate, finely chopped

2 tablespoons Grand Marnier
Unsweetened cocoa

Bring heavy cream and lavender to boil. Boil 1 minute and strain over chopped chocolate in bowl. Add Grand Marnier and stir occasionally until chocolate is completely melted. Cool in refrigerator 3 hours until completely set.

With warm spoon, roll truffle mixture into cherry-size balls. Then roll truffles in sifted unsweetened cocoa or dip in melted chocolate.
Makes approximately 12 truffles.

Chocolate Pumpkin Cake

Fine dry bread crumbs
2 ¾ cups flour
¾ cup unsweetened cocoa
2 teaspoons baking powder
1 teaspoon baking soda
1 ½ teaspoons cinnamon
½ teaspoon ginger
½ teaspoon salt
¼ teaspoon ground cloves
¼ teaspoon nutmeg

1 cup softened butter or
   margarine
2 cups granulated sugar
1 ½ teaspoons vanilla
4 eggs
1 can (1 pound) pumpkin (1 ¾
   cups)
1 ½ cups coarsely chopped
   pecans
Confectioners sugar

Thoroughly grease a 3-quart fluted tube pan. Sprinkle with bread crumbs. Set aside.

Mix together the flour, cocoa, baking powder, baking soda, cinnamon, ginger, salt, cloves and nutmeg. Set aside.

In large bowl, cream butter with sugar and vanilla. Add eggs, one at a time, beating well after each. Stir in half the flour mixture, then the pumpkin, then remaining flour mixture just until well blended. Stir in pecans.

Turn batter into the prepared pan and smooth the top of the batter. Bake in a 325 degree oven for 80 to 90 minutes, or until toothpick inserted in the middle of cake comes out clean.

Remove from oven; let stand on rack 15 minutes. Invert on rack and cool completely. Remove pan, cover and let stand several hours or overnight before serving. Dust with confectioners sugar or frost with your favorite chocolate frosting.   Serves 10 to 12.

Harvest Apple Cake

1 cup golden raisins
½ cup Late Harvest
   Gewürztraminer or Riesling
2 ¾ cups flour
1 ½ teaspoons baking soda
1 ½ teaspoons cinnamon
½ teaspoon baking powder
½ teaspoon salt
½ teaspoon nutmeg

¼ teaspoon allspice
¼ teaspoon ginger
¾ cup sweet butter, at room
   temperature
1 ¾ cups sugar
3 large or 4 medium eggs,
   beaten
1 ¾ cups unsweetened
   applesauce

Soak raisins in gently boiling wine for 10 minutes. Mix together the flour, baking soda, cinnamon, baking powder, salt, nutmeg, allspice and ginger.

Beat butter and sugar together. In alternating fashion, add eggs and flour mixture to butter mixture. Fold in raisins and applesauce.

Pour into a buttered and floured bundt pan. Bake at 350 degrees for 1 hour or until done.   Serves 6 to 8.

Serve with a Late Harvest Zinfandel.

Persimmon Walnut Cake
with Champagne Sea Foam Sauce

1 ½ cups coarsely chopped
  walnuts
1 ½ cups bittersweet chocolate
  chunks (or chocolate chips)
3 cups flour
3 teaspoons baking powder
1 teaspoon ground cinnamon
1 teaspoon ground ginger (or
  1 tablespoon minced
  candied ginger)

½ teaspoon freshly grated
  nutmeg
1 cup sweet butter, softened
  (2 cubes)
2 cups sugar
1 ½ cups puréed persimmon
  or pumpkin
4 eggs
¾ cup Blanc de Noir
  Champagne

Toss the walnuts and chocolate in ½ cup of the flour. Sift the flour, baking powder, cinnamon, ginger and nutmeg together. Set aside. Cream the butter and sugar in a mixing bowl until fluffy. Beat in the pureé and then the eggs, one at a time. Fold in the dry ingredients, alternating with the Champagne. Stir in the nuts and chocolate. Pour the batter into an ungreased 10-inch tube or bundt pan. Bake 1 hour and 15 minutes at 325 degrees. Cool and remove from the pan. Serve in slices with Sea Foam Sauce or whipped cream.

Serves 12.

CHAMPAGNE SEA FOAM SAUCE:
2 tablespoons butter, softened
2 tablespoons flour
½ cup sugar
1 egg yolk

½ cup Blanc de Noir
  Champagne
1 teaspoon vanilla
1 egg white, beaten medium

Whisk together the butter, flour and sugar in a saucepan. Beat the egg yolk into the Champagne, and stir into the butter mixture. Cook over low heat, stirring constantly, until thickened. Cool. Just before serving, add the vanilla, and fold in the beaten egg white. Makes 1 ½ cups.

Serve with Champagne.

California Brandied Fruit Cake

2 ½ cups raisins (combine golden and black)
2 ½ cups chopped dried figs (black mission)
1 cup Brandy
1 ½ cups butter
2 ½ cups brown sugar
1 tablespoon cinnamon
½ tablespoon allspice

½ tablespoon nutmeg
½ tablespoon ground cloves
5 eggs
1 ¼ cups raspberry or blackberry jam
5 cups unbleached white flour
1 tablespoon baking soda
2 ½ cups chopped, toasted walnuts or pecans

Butter and flour 4 large loaf pans.

Soak the raisins and figs in the Brandy for at least 2 hours. Reserve Brandy. Cream butter, then add brown sugar, cinnamon, allspice, nutmeg and cloves. Cream until light. Add eggs, beating after each addition. Stir in jam. Transfer to a large mixing bowl. Sift the flour together with the baking soda, and add to ingredients in the mixing bowl. Fold in nuts and soaked raisins and figs. Pour into prepared pans.

Bake in a 325 degree oven for 40 minutes to 1 hour. While still warm, brush each cake liberally on all sides with Brandy.

When cool, wrap in plastic wrap or parchment paper and keep in a tightly closed tin.

If you wish to age the cakes, they may be periodically brushed with more Brandy. The cakes can be made as early as September to be served at Christmas time.   Makes 4 large loaves.

Pear Gingerbread Upside Down Cake

⅓ cup plus 2 tablespoons
    butter
2 tablespoons brown sugar
3 pears, peeled and halved
⅓ cup sugar
1 egg
½ cup molasses

1 ½ cups flour
¾ teaspoon baking soda
1 teaspoon cinnamon
1 teaspoon ground ginger
¼ teaspoon ground cloves
½ teaspoon salt
½ cup hot water

Melt 2 tablespoons of the butter with brown sugar and put in the bottom of a square 9-inch by 9-inch pan, along with the pears cut side down.

To make the batter, mix the remaining ⅓ cup butter, sugar, egg, molasses, flour, baking soda, cinnamon, ginger, cloves, salt and hot water together.

Pour batter over the pears and bake 50 minutes at 350 degrees. Cool 10 minutes and invert onto serving platter.   Serves 6 to 8.

Poached Pears in Zinfandel

3 cups Zinfandel
1 ½ cups sugar
1 vanilla bean, split in half
   lengthwise
¼ of a cinnamon stick
2 peppercorns

1 clove
1 thyme sprig
4 mint sprigs
Zest and juice of 1 lemon
4 ripe but firm Comice, Bartlett
   or Bosc pears

Mix the Zinfandel, sugar, vanilla bean, cinnamon, peppercorns, clove, thyme and lemon zest in a sauce pan. Bring to a boil and simmer for 5 minutes. Carefully peel, core and cut the pears in half. Dip each half in the lemon juice before immediately immersing it in the simmering syrup. Simmer for 8 to 10 minutes, or until a small knife inserted in the middle of the pear meets a slight resistance. Carefully pour everything into a bowl, letting it cool (several hours will do, but overnight is best).

Take out two halves at a time. Starting at the bottom of each pear, slice them ¾ of the way up (lengthwise), enabling you to fan out the halves. Place the two uncut tops of the pears together, strain a little of the syrup over them and garnish with mint sprigs.   Serves 4.

Poached Figs over Ice Cream

1 cup Late Harvest Zinfandel
1 tablespoon honey
½ teaspoon chopped fresh
   thyme leaves

½ teaspoon grated fresh
   lemon peel
½ teaspoon vanilla
½ pound dried Calmyrna figs

In a saucepan, bring the wine, honey, thyme, lemon peel and vanilla to a boil. Simmer for 3 to 4 minutes. Set aside.

Stem figs, cut in half, and slice each fig half into thin strips. Add the figs to the wine mixture, cover and simmer for 5 to 10 minutes until figs are soft.

Serve the figs and syrup over vanilla ice cream.   Serves 4.

Ginger Apple Tart

1 9-inch pie crust
2 tablespoons brown sugar
1 teaspoon cinnamon
3 apples, peeled, cored and sliced in even pieces
½ cup sugar
4 tablespoons flour
2 eggs
2 tablespoons minced candied ginger
½ cup melted butter
Cinnamon, for garnish

Preheat oven to 425 degrees. Prepare pie crust in a 9-inch tart pan. Sprinkle the brown sugar and cinnamon over the bottom of the crust. Bake for 10 minutes. Remove and cool slightly. Reduce oven temperature to 375 degrees. Place sliced apples in crust in even rows.

Combine sugar, flour, eggs and ginger, mixing well. Slowly whisk in melted butter. Pour this filling mixture over apples. Sprinkle a bit of cinnamon over pie for color. Bake at 375 degrees for 1 hour, or until golden brown.

Serve with a scoop of vanilla ice cream or a dash of whipped cream.
Serves 6.

Peppernut Cookies

1 cup brown sugar, packed
4 tablespoons butter, softened
1 egg
1 teaspoon Brandy
1 ¾ cups flour
¼ teaspoon baking soda
¼ teaspoon cloves
¼ teaspoon ginger
¼ teaspoon cinnamon
¼ teaspoon pepper

Cream together the butter and brown sugar. Stir in egg and Brandy. Mix together the flour, baking soda, cloves, ginger, cinnamon and pepper. Add to the butter mixture, mixing with hands. Shape into balls and place 1 inch apart on baking sheet.

Bake in 375 degree oven for 8 minutes or until lightly browned. Keep tightly covered in a tin or store in deep freeze.   Makes 70.

Ginger Pear Tart

CRUST:

8 tablespoons sweet butter, chilled

1 cup flour

1 tablespoon sugar

3-4 drops almond extract

1 tablespoon water

To make the crust, mix all ingredients with pastry blender or finger tips, mixing uniformly. Roll into circle about 1 ½ inches larger than a 9 or 10-inch tart pan. Fit crust into pan, fluting and crimping top of crust to pan. Bake crust at 425 degrees for 10 minutes.

FILLING:

½ cup sugar

4 tablespoons flour

2 eggs

2 tablespoons chopped candied ginger

½ cup melted unsalted butter

3 pears peeled, cored and sliced into fan shape (can use apples or seedless grapes)

Combine sugar, flour, eggs and ginger. Slowly whisk in melted butter. Arrange pears in crust and pour filling mixture around pears. Bake at 375 degrees for 1 hour, or until golden.   Serves 6 to 8.

Chocolate Bread Pudding

2 eggs

1 ½ cups fine, soft bread crumbs

3 cups milk, scalded*

1 tablespoon butter

⅔ cup sugar

1 teaspoon cinnamon

¼ teaspoon salt

3 squares unsweetened chocolate, melted

1 teaspoon vanilla

½ cup semi-sweet chocolate chips

Whipped cream

Beat eggs, add bread crumbs, milk, butter, sugar, cinnamon and salt. Mix well. Add melted chocolate and vanilla, folding in chocolate chips. Pour into a greased baking dish and bake in a 325 degrees until firm, about 40 minutes. Test center of pudding to see if it is done. Serve hot or cold with whipped cream.   Serves 6 to 8.

Heated to just below boiling point, then removed from heat.

Caramel Apple Tart

2 ready-prepared pie crusts
3 to 3 ½ cups thinly sliced
   apples (4 medium apples)
½ cup sugar
¾ teaspoon cinnamon
½ teaspoon nutmeg
2 tablespoons flour
4 tablespoons golden raisins

4 tablespoons chopped
  pecans
½ teaspoon grated lemon peel
2 teaspoons lemon juice
12 caramel candies
1 tablespoon butter
2 tablespoons milk

Heat oven to 400 degrees. Place a cookie sheet in the oven to preheat.

Prepare 1 of the pie crusts according to package directions, using a 10-inch tart pan with removable bottom.

In a large bowl, combine apples, sugar, cinnamon, nutmeg and flour. Toss gently to coat. Add raisins, pecans, lemon peel and lemon juice. Gently toss. Spoon into crust.

Make a lattice top by cutting the second pie crust into ½-inch slices. Arrange strips in lattice pattern over filling. Seal edges and trim off excess pastry.

Place tart on preheated cookie sheet. Cover edge of crust with foil after 15 to 20 minutes of baking to prevent excessive browning. Bake for 50 to 60 minutes or until apples are tender and crust is golden brown. Remove tart and cool.

While tart is cooling, combine caramels, butter and milk in a small saucepan. Stir over medium-low heat until caramels melt and become a smooth syrup. Drizzle caramel over tart and allow caramel to set before serving. Serves 8.

Chocolate Chip Pumpkin Pie

2 eggs, slightly beaten
¾ cup sugar
1 ½ teaspoons ground
  cinnamon
½ teaspoon ground nutmeg
½ teaspoon ground ginger
¼ teaspoon ground allspice
¼ teaspoon ground cloves
½ teaspoon salt
1 can (2 cups) pumpkin

2 cans (6 ounces each)
  evaporated milk
1 prepared pie crust
1 egg white, unbeaten
¼ cup finely chopped pecans
2 cups semi-sweet chocolate
  chips
8 whole pecan halves
Whipped cream
Dash of nutmeg

Preheat oven to 400 degrees.

To make the filling, combine the eggs, sugar, cinnamon, nutmeg, ginger, allspice, cloves, salt, pumpkin and milk in a large bowl until mixture is smooth.

Lightly brush pie crust with egg white. Sprinkle chopped pecans on the bottom of the pie crust. Then sprinkle chocolate chips. Fill with pumpkin filling. Gently arrange pecan halves on filling around edge of pie.

Bake for 55 to 60 minutes or until tip of sharp knife inserted in center comes out clean. Let cool on wire rack. Serve garnished with whipped cream. Top cream with a sprinkle of nutmeg before serving. Makes 6 to 8 servings.

Lemon Curd Tart with Hazelnut Crust, Fresh Strawberries and Raspberries

1 ready-prepared pie crust
2 tablespoons toasted and
   finely chopped hazelnuts
2 large lemons
½ cup butter
1 cup fine sugar
3 eggs, lightly beaten

1 pint fresh strawberries
1 pint fresh raspberries
¼ cup coarsely chopped
   pistachio nuts
Powdered sugar for dusting
Lemon zest for garnish

Heat oven to 375 degrees. Roll out crust and place in a tart pan. Fold edges of crust over to form a fluted crust edge. Sprinkle chopped hazelnuts on bottom of crust and pat gently into crust. Bake in oven according to package directions (10 to 15 minutes) or until lightly browned. Remove from oven and cool at room temperature.

To prepare lemon curd, remove zest from lemons with a fine grater; set aside. Squeeze juice from the lemons. Melt butter in a saucepan over medium heat and gradually stir in the sugar. Add eggs, lemon juice and zest, and continue cooking. Stir until thickened, then remove from heat and cool.

Stem, rinse and dry the strawberries. Cut in half. Rinse and dry the raspberries.

Evenly spread the lemon curd inside the tart shell. Decoratively arrange the strawberries and raspberries on top of the lemon curd. Dust the tart lightly with powdered sugar. Sprinkle the tart with the chopped pistachios. Garnish each plate with lemon zest.

Serves 6.

Enjoy with a Moscato wine.

Biscotti

6 eggs
2 cups sugar
3 cups sifted flour
3 teaspoons baking powder
Grated lemon rind
1 ½ cubes melted butter
1 teaspoon vanilla

2 teaspoons almond extract
1 teaspoon (or more) anise
  seed
1 teaspoon anise extract
1 jigger Brandy
1 cup chopped almonds

Cream together eggs, sugar, flour and baking powder. Add the remaining ingredients. Pour onto a greased cookie sheet with edges. Bake at 350 degrees for 30 to 40 minutes.

Cut into serving-size biscuits and place each piece on its side on cookie sheet. The Biscotti will not all fit on one cookie sheet. Return to oven for a few minutes to brown slowly so they are nice and crunchy. Don't forget to toast both sides.   Makes 25 to 30.

Perfect for dunking into Zinfandel or Cabernet.

This recipe for Biscotti Cookies also appeared in our two previous California Wine Country Cookbooks, and is included in this book because of the response it received. VMH

Brandied Bananas

3 ripe but firm bananas
½ cup orange juice
½ cup Brandy
¼ cup brown sugar
½ teaspoon cinnamon

¼ cup grated coconut
3 tablespoons butter or
  margarine
½ cup whipping cream

Peel bananas, slice lengthwise, and arrange cut side down in glass baking plate. Cover with the orange juice and Brandy. Sprinkle brown sugar, cinnamon, and grated coconut on top, and dot with butter. Bake in a 350 degree oven for 20 minutes. Serve with whipped cream.   Serves 6.

Black Forest Brownies

½ cup butter
4 ounces unsweetened
  chocolate
4 eggs
2 cups sugar
1 tablespoon Brandy

2 teaspoons cinnamon
½ teaspoon nutmeg
½ teaspoon salt
1 ¼ cups flour
1 cup chopped walnuts
1 cup chopped glazed cherries

Heat oven to 350 degrees. Melt butter and chocolate in a small saucepan. Let cool.

Break eggs into a large bowl and beat. Add sugar, Brandy, cinnamon and nutmeg. Mix well. Gradually add flour and salt, and beat until smooth. Mix in chocolate mixture. Add walnuts and cherries. Spread mixture in a 9 × 13-inch greased cake pan. Bake for 35 minutes. Cool before cutting into 2-inch squares.

Makes approximately 24 brownies.

Spicy Chocolate Macaroons

1 ½ cups coconut flakes
½ cup sugar
3 tablespoons flour
⅛ teaspoon salt
1 teaspoon cinnamon

½ teaspoon nutmeg
2 squares unsweetened
  chocolate, melted
2 egg whites
1 teaspoon vanilla

Combine coconut, sugar, flour, salt, cinnamon and nutmeg in a bowl and mix. Stir in chocolate, egg whites and vanilla. Mix well.

Drop by teaspoonful on lightly greased baking sheets.

Bake at 325 degrees for 20 to 25 minutes, or until edges brown. Remove from baking sheets and enjoy.   Makes about 18 to 20.

Fresh Thyme and Tomato Sorbet

6 ounces sugar
7 ounces water
2 ounces glucose (heavy white
  corn syrup)
24 medium tomatoes
Salt and freshly ground pepper
4 ½ cups fresh or canned
  tomato juice

Juice of ½ lemon, strained
1 teaspoon chopped fresh
  thyme
⅛ teaspoon cayenne pepper
8 sprigs fresh thyme

To make the syrup, combine sugar, water and glucose in a sauce pan and bring to a boil, stirring occasionally. Boil for 3 minutes, skimming the surface of any white foam that may appear. Strain and set aside to cool.

Blanch the tomatoes by putting them into a sauce pan of boiling, salted water for 10 seconds and then immerse immediately into cold water to stop them from cooking further. Skin them, cut ⅓ off the stem end of the tomato and a thin slice off the other end so it will stand firmly. Remove the seeds and cores, season the inside with salt and freshly ground pepper. Place upside down on a plate in the refrigerator.

In a bowl mix the tomato juice, lemon juice, cooled syrup, chopped thyme and cayenne pepper with salt and freshly ground black pepper to taste (if the mixture is still a little too acidic, add a little more salt to balance it).

Pour into an ice cream machine and churn for 10 to 20 minutes. This will vary depending on the machine. The sherbet should be smooth and velvety. Fill the finished sherbet into the tomato shells. Place 3 per person onto a chilled plate and decorate with thyme sprigs.   Serves 8.

Custard-Rhubarb Pie

BOTTOM FILLING
1 ready-to-bake pie crust (9
   inches)
4 cups diced rhubarb
½ cup sugar
½ teaspoon grated lemon peel
½ teaspoon cinnamon
¼ teaspoon powdered ginger
2 tablespoons flour

TOP CUSTARD FILLING
1 cup heavy cream
2 eggs, beaten
½ cup sugar
1 teaspoon vanilla
¼ teaspoon cinnamon
¼ teaspoon ginger

Preheat oven to 350 degrees. Bake pie crust according to package directions to lightly browned. Put rhubarb, sugar, lemon peel and spices into a saucepan with 2 tablespoons water. Simmer on low. (Rhubarb contains a lot of water and it will produce sufficient juices to continue cooking until tender.) Cook no more than 10 minutes. Add the flour and stir until juices thicken. Set aside.

Pour the rhubarb into the pie shell. Mix all the custard filling ingredients well and pour over rhubarb. Bake at 350 degrees for 40 to 50 minutes, until custard is golden brown and set in the center. Cover the pie crust edges with foil after 15 to 20 minutes to prevent edge from getting too dark.
                                            Serves 6.

Strawberry-Rhubarb Crisp

4 cups strawberries, cleaned
   and cut into halves or
   quarters
3 cups sliced rhubarb, ¼-inch
   wide
¾ cup sugar

½ cup plus 1 tablespoon flour
1 tablespoon cornstarch
½ teaspoon nutmeg
½ cup rolled oats
½ cup butter (softened)

Heat oven to 400 degrees. Grease an 8 × 8-inch baking dish. Mix strawberries and rhubarb with the sugar, 1 tablespoon of the flour, cornstarch and nutmeg. Arrange in the baking dish. Mix remaining ½ cup flour, rolled oats and butter to make the topping. Cover evenly over fruit. Bake about 40 minutes, until fruit is bubbly and topping is lightly browned. Cool slightly and serve with ice cream or whipped cream.
                                         Serves 4 to 6.

Salsas
Sauces &
Condiments

THE HERBS & SPICES COOKBOOK

Chile Banana Salsa

2 large bananas, peeled and
  diced
½ cup seeded and minced red
  bell pepper
½ cup seeded and minced
  green bell pepper
1 jalapeño chile, seeded and
  minced
1 tablespoon minced fresh
  ginger

3 scallions, chopped fine
¼ cup chopped fresh cilantro
3 tablespoons fresh lime juice
2 tablespoons brown sugar
¼ teaspoon ground cardamon
1 tablespoon olive oil
Salt and freshly ground
  pepper

Combine all of the ingredients in a bowl, and gently toss to mix. Correct the seasonings if needed, adding salt, lime juice, or sugar. The salsa should be sweet and sour.

Refrigerate, covered, until serving time. For best flavor, serve within 2 hours of making.   Makes 3 cups.

A perfect salsa for barbecued or grilled fish or shrimp.

Cranberry Chile Salsa

1 bag (12-ounces) cranberries
  (frozen can be used)
2-3 cloves of garlic
1-2 jalapeño chilies
4 tablespoons finely chopped
  cilantro

3 green onions, minced
⅓ cup lime juice
  (approximately 3 limes)
½ cup sugar
Salt and pepper

Boil cranberries in 1 quart of water for 1 minute. Drain well. Mince garlic, then seed and mince jalapeños. Combine with the cilantro, onions, and cranberries in a large bowl. Mix, add lime juice, sugar, and salt and pepper.

Peach N' Pineapple Salsa

2 ripe, but firm peaches,
  peeled, pitted and diced
1 cup diced fresh pineapple
½ medium red onion, peeled
  and minced
½ cup canned pineapple juice
¼ cup fresh lime juice

1 tablespoon minced fresh
  ginger
1 teaspoon ground cumin
1 teaspoon ground coriander
1 teaspoon brown sugar
½ teaspoon salt
¼ teaspoon cayenne pepper

Combine the peaches, pineapple, onion and remaining ingredients in a bowl; mix lightly. Cover and refrigerate.   Makes 4 cups.

This is a versatile salsa that would enhance fish or chicken dishes.

Black Bean-Corn Salsa

3 medium-size ears of fresh
  corn, cooked
1 Anaheim chile, peeled,
  cored, seeded and chopped
½ cup chopped red onion
1 can (16 ounces) black
  beans, rinsed and drained

3 plum tomatoes, chopped
2 tablespoons fresh lemon
  juice
1 tablespoon fresh lime juice
¼ teaspoon salt
¼ teaspoon pepper

Cut the corn kernels from the cobs. Mix in a bowl with remaining ingredients.   Makes 4 cups.

A very good salsa for a barbecue or picnic.

Classic Salsa

1 ½ jalapeño chilies, seeded
  and cored
1 tablespoon minced garlic
1 cup minced scallions
4 ripe tomatoes, seeded and
  cut in large pieces

Juice of 1 lemon
½ cup stemmed and coarsely
  chopped fresh cilantro
¾ teaspoon salt
¼ teaspoon freshly ground
  pepper

Put jalapeño and garlic in a food processor fitted with a steel blade. Pulse until a fine paste is formed. Add the scallions, pulsing on and off several times. Add the tomatoes. Chop until fine, pulsing on and off.

Transfer mixture to a serving bowl, and stir in the lemon juice, cilantro, salt and pepper. To blend flavors, cover and let sit for 30 minutes at room temperature.   Makes 3 cups.

A recipe for the true salsa lover!

Salsa Santa Fe

40 tomatillos
2 bunches cilantro, chopped
1 medium onion, finely
  chopped
4 serrano chilies, seeded and
  thinly chopped

5 jalapeños, quartered,
  seeded and finely chopped
2 tablespoons ground cumin
Juice from 1 lime
2 cloves garlic, crushed
Salt and pepper

Soak tomatillos in warm water for 5 minutes, remove husks, and boil until tender, about 10 minutes. Drain excess water. Blend or purée tomatillos, and add the rest of the ingredients, blending well.
                    Serves 8 to 10.

Serve with grilled meats and Cabernet Sauvignon.

Salsa Carib

6 Roma tomatoes, peeled, seeded and diced
1 papaya, peeled, seeded and diced
1 small red onion, diced
½ cup sliced black olives
2 tablespoons finely chopped fresh mint
Zest and juice of 2 limes

2 tablespoons dark brown sugar
1 teaspoon cumin
1 teaspoon chile powder
1 teaspoon crushed red pepper flakes
½ teaspoon salt
1 teaspoon Worcestershire sauce

Combine the tomatoes, papaya and onion in a bowl. Place the mixture in a food processor or blender to purée. Return the purée to the bowl. Add the remaining ingredients and stir to blend well.

Set aside for 1 hour or more. The salsa is best when served at room temperature. Makes 4 cups.

A versatile salsa that can be served with chicken, fish or meat.

Cilantro Sauce

4 plum tomatoes, chopped
1 cup chopped cilantro
4 green onions, roughly sliced
1 tablespoon lemon juice
¼ teaspoon ground cinnamon
¼ teaspoon ground cumin

2 small green jalapeño chilies, seeded and chopped
¼ teaspoon ground turmeric
¼ teaspoon ground cloves
Salt and pepper

Process all ingredients in a food processor or blender until a smooth paste forms. Add more lemon juice or a little water to achieve desired consistency. Makes 1 cup.

A piquant salsa great with steak or hamburgers.

Mushroom Cream Sauce with Tarragon

Serve with unseasoned chicken breasts which have been grilled, sautéed or broiled

1 pound button mushrooms, thinly sliced
4 ounces (1 stick) unsalted butter
1 cup chicken stock (unsalted or low-salt)
⅔ cup heavy cream
2 tablespoons finely chopped parsley

2 tablespoons finely chopped fresh tarragon, or 1 teaspoon dried

GARNISH:
⅓ cup pine nuts (pignoli)
1 tablespoon unsalted butter

Sauté the mushrooms in butter over medium heat, stirring frequently until tender. Add chicken stock and continue cooking, stirring occasionally, until liquid is reduce by half. Add cream; continue cooking and stirring until liquid is again reduced by half.

Add parsley and tarragon and cook briefly, stirring to blend flavors. For garnish, sauté pine nuts in butter over medium heat until golden brown on both sides. Sprinkle over sauce on each serving.

Makes 2 cups, serves 8.

This recipe was developed to enhance the flavor of chicken and to complement the rich, full-bodied flavor of a smooth Chardonnay.

Mediterranean Medley

Serve with unseasoned chicken breasts, grilled, sautéed or broiled.

½ cup finely chopped onions
3 cloves garlic, finely minced
3 tablespoons olive oil
2 green onions, thinly sliced
(white part plus 2 inches of
green)
2 medium carrots, very finely
chopped
2 medium unpeeled zucchini,
very finely chopped

½ tablespoon lemon juice
½ teaspoon lemon zest
3 sun-dried tomatoes (oil
packed) finely chopped
2 tablespoons finely chopped
fresh basil, or 1 teaspoon
dried

Sauté the onions and garlic in olive oil over low heat until they begin to soften. Add green onions, carrots and zucchini; cook slowly until tender. Stir in lemon juice, lemon zest and sun-dried tomatoes. Cook briefly, stirring to blend flavors. Add salt if necessary. Add basil at last minute.   Makes 2 cups, serves 8.

Blend Mediterranean flavors with the crisp fresh acidity of a Sauvignon Blanc!

Wild Mushroom Sauce with Rosemary and Bacon

Serve with unseasoned beef, grilled, sautéed or broiled.

¼ cup olive oil
½ cup finely chopped bacon
1 medium red bell pepper,
  finely chopped
6 medium cloves garlic,
  minced
2 cups finely chopped fresh
  shiitake mushrooms* (6
  large mushrooms, stems
  removed)

¼ teaspoon very finely
  chopped fresh or dried
  rosemary
¼ cup unsalted or low-salt
  beef broth

In olive oil, sauté the bacon over low heat until it begins to soften. Add red bell pepper and garlic, sauté slowly, stirring frequently, until well coated with oil and slightly softened. Add mushrooms; mix well and cover pan. Cook over low heat, stirring occasionally, until mushrooms have released their liquid. Uncover pan, add rosemary and broth, and continue cooking until liquid is almost all evaporated.

Makes 2 cups, serves 8.

*Regular cultivated mushrooms may be substituted, but flavor will be less intense.

The rich full flavors of Cabernet Sauvignon stand up nicely to the meaty black mushrooms and its mildly herbal flavors match well with the red bell pepper and rosemary.

Spicy Cherry Sauce

⅓ cup finely minced green
  onions
½ cube butter (2 ounces)
1 ½ cups chicken broth
  (unsalted or low salt)
⅔ cup cream
1 ½ cups finely chopped
  canned red cherries,
  reserving ¼ cup juice from
  the can

1 ½ teaspoons finely ground
  black pepper
1 ½ teaspoons prepared Dijon
  mustard
1 ½ teaspoons cinnamon
1 teaspoon lemon juice

Sauté the onions in butter over medium heat, stirring frequently, until soft and translucent. Add chicken broth and continue cooking, stirring occasionally, until liquid is reduced by half. Add cream and continue cooking and stirring until liquid is again reduced by half. Add remaining ingredients and continue cooking, stirring occasionally, until sauce is thick and creamy.

Makes approximately 2 cups.

Serve with chicken, turkey or veal.

Zinfandel Peppercorn Sauce

¼ cup mixed whole
  peppercorns
¼ cup Zinfandel

1 tablespoon sweet-hot mustard
1 tablespoon balsamic vinegar
½ cup extra virgin olive oil

Grind the peppercorns in spice grinder, or use a mortar and pestle. Bring Zinfandel to a slight boil. Lower heat and simmer until wine is reduced to 1 tablespoon. Blend peppercorns, mustard, vinegar and reduced Zinfandel in a food processor.

Add olive oil, slowly, while processor is on. Continue blending until sauce is thickened, about 1 to 2 minutes. Sauce will separate if it gets too warm! Refrigerate until ready to use.   Makes ½ cup.

Picante Red Wine Sauce

1 ½ cups red wine
½ cup brown sugar
½ teaspoon grated lemon peel

½ teaspoon grated orange peel
1 jalapeño chile, seeded and
 minced

Heat all ingredients until simmering gently and sugar is dissolved. Continue to simmer for 20 to 25 minutes until chile is soft.

Makes 1 ½ cups.

A perfect sauce for ham.

Hot Tomato Sauce

1 red bell pepper, seeded and
 minced
1 medium onion, minced
2 celery stalks, cut into 3-inch
 lengths

1 can (8 ounces) tomato
 sauce
2 small poblano chilies,
 seeded and chopped

Cook all ingredients together, simmering, for 15 to 20 minutes. Add water, if necessary, to cover vegetables. Allow to cool. Place in a blender and blend until smooth. Reheat and serve.

Makes 1 ½ cups.

This sauce is especially good with chicken or other poultry.

Red Onion Marmalade

4 red onions
3 tablespoons unsalted butter
2 cups Cabernet Sauvignon
2 tablespoons balsamic
   vinegar

2 tablespoons Creme de
   Cassis
Salt and freshly ground pepper

Peel and slice the onions very thin. Melt the butter in a large heavy pan, and add the onions. Cook very slowly over low heat, stirring occasionally, until onions are soft. This will take about ½ hour.

Raise the heat to high, add the wine, vinegar and Cassis; bring to a boil. Reduce heat to a simmer, and cook until the liquid has been entirely absorbed into the onions. Season to taste with salt and freshly ground pepper.   Serves 8.

Serve with lamb or beef.

Pearl Onion Compote

2 pounds pearl onions, peeled
¾ cup golden raisins
½ cup peanut oil
⅓ cup wine vinegar
⅓ cup tomato paste
6 cloves garlic, peeled and
   crushed

2 sprigs parsley
2 springs fresh thyme
6 leaves of sage
2 bay leaves
Chardonnay (or dry white
   wine) to cover
Salt and pepper

Combine all ingredients in a stainless steel pot. Bring to simmer over low heat. Cover and simmer until tender. Remove bay leaves. Cool. If compote is too runny, strain and cook liquid slowly until syrupy, then combine with onions and chill.

Serve at room temperature as a salad on a bed of young greens, or as a garnish to duck or pheasant.
                    Serves 6 as salad, 8 to 10 as garnish.

Minted Red Onion Blackberry Relish

Serve with unseasoned beef, grilled, sautéed or broiled.

4 tablespoons olive oil
8 cups thinly sliced red onions
(4 large or 6 medium onions)
1 cup fresh or frozen
blackberries

2 teaspoons finely chopped
fresh mint
½ teaspoon finely ground
black pepper

In olive oil, sauté onions over low heat until coated with oil. Cover pan and cook slowly, stirring frequently, until onions are soft and translucent. Add blackberries and cook, mashing them slightly until fruit is well blended. Add mint and black pepper and stir briefly to blend flavors. Makes 2 cups, serves 8.

Serve with a Zinfandel.

Brandied Cranberry Apple Relish

4 tart apples, peeled and diced
2 pounds fresh cranberries
2 cups sugar
1 cup golden raisins
1 cup orange juice
1 medium onion, chopped fine

2 tablespoons grated orange
rind
2 teaspoons cinnamon
½ teaspoon nutmeg
½ cup Brandy

Mix together all ingredients except Brandy in a sauce pan.

Bring to boil, then reduce heat and simmer slowly for 45 minutes, stirring occasionally, so it will not stick. Cook until thick. Stir in Brandy. remove from heat. Cool.

This relish is especially good with poultry or pork.

Dried Fruit Chutney

1 pound dried apricots,
  chopped
1 cup raisins
1 cup dried papaya, pineapple
  or other sweet dried fruit,
  chopped
½ pound chopped preserved
  or candied ginger
2 cups diced onions

2 ½ cups cider vinegar
2 ½ cups dark brown sugar
2 teaspoons salt
1 tablespoon dry mustard
1 teaspoon cayenne
½ teaspoon turmeric
Grated rind and juice of 1
  orange

Combine all the ingredients together in a large non-reactive pot and bring to a boil. Reduce the heat and simmer until the chutney has thickened. Stir occasionally to prevent scorching. That's it.

Makes 3 ½ cups.

This is a sharp, hot chutney that is very easy to make, and will add zest when served with beef, veal, chicken or turkey.

Apple Chutney

Chutney is a sweet and sour condiment, usually fruit based. This is a very simple, easy to make recipe, great with roast pork or chicken.

5 medium apples, cored and
  chopped fine (about 7 cups)
2 cups brown sugar
3 to 5 slices of fresh ginger,
  each the size of a quarter

1 ¾ cups cider vinegar
¼ teaspoon white pepper
¼ teaspoon ground mace
⅛ teaspoon ground clove

Bring all ingredients to a boil, then reduce to a simmer. Stir occasionally and continue cooking over low heat until the apples are very soft and the liquid is almost completely evaporated and absorbed. Remove the ginger slices and chill before serving.

Makes about 3 ½ cups.

Herbed and Spiced Butters

There is probably no easier way to transform an ordinary dish into something truly special than by whipping up a herbed or spiced butter to serve with it.

Blackberry-Mint Butter

2 cups fresh or frozen
  blackberries (if frozen, drain
  off excess liquid)

¼ cup fresh chopped mint
½ pound sweet butter at room
  temperature

Combine all ingredients in a food processor and pulse a few times to get mixture going. Then, just let the machine run until all ingredients are well mixed together. Butter will be a rich, dark purple color. Preparation time: 5 minutes

Yields ½ pound, serves 10 people.

Walnut-Mustard Butter

1 ½ cups walnuts
¼ cup whole grain mustard
Salt and pepper

½ pound sweet butter at room
  temperature

Follow the same procedures for the Blackberry-Mint Butter recipe above. This time, the butter will be light brown in color. Preparation time: 5 minutes.

Yields ½ pound, serves 10 people.

Serve either or both of these butters with grilled New York steak, salmon or chicken.

Cajun Spice Butter

1 pound sweet butter, at room
  temperature
1 teaspoon cayenne
4 teaspoons paprika
4 teaspoons garlic powder
4 teaspoons onion powder
4 teaspoons chili powder

2 teaspoons coriander
2 teaspoons cumin
2 teaspoons Italian herbs
1 teaspoon oregano
1 teaspoon black pepper
1 teaspoon salt

Combine all ingredients in a mixer and blend thoroughly. Serve with grilled trout, chicken or rib eye steak. Preparation time: 10 minutes.
Yield: 1 pound, serves 20 people.

If you desire a little more heat from the butter, add more cayenne and chili powder.

Herbed Garlic Butter

¼ cup chopped fresh parsley
¼ cup chopped fresh mint
  leaves
2 tablespoons chopped fresh
  basil leaves

2 cloves garlic, chopped
¼ teaspoon black pepper
½ pound (2 cups) butter, at
  room temperature

Combine all ingredients in a food processor and pulse a few times to get mixture going. Then, just let the machine run until all ingredients are well mixed. Butter will be a fresh green color.
Yields ½ pound, serves 10 people.

Serve with steak. chicken or fish.

216

Here are some easy herbed and spiced butters to use in your everyday cooking, with the foods they will complement best.

Your basic measurement is ½ cup butter, softened at room temperature (never heat the butter to soften). Add herbs and/or spices as specified, blending well.

BASIL BUTTER
1 teaspoon basil
1 ½ teaspoons grated onion

Hamburgers, Italian green beans

CHILI BUTTER
½ teaspoon crumbled dried basil leaves
1 teaspoon chili powder

Hot corn, tomatoes, chicken, frankfurters, fish

CHIVE BUTTER
1/16 teaspoon ground black pepper
1 ½ tablespoons freeze-dried chives
Lemon juice to taste
Salt

Cabbage, carrots, potatoes, corn, green beans, peas, fish, chicken, liver, mushrooms, grilled meats, oysters, turnips, ham or egg salad sandwiches

CURRY BUTTER
1 teaspoon curry powder
Dusting of ground black pepper and paprika

Potatoes, spinach, cauliflower, corn, chicken, fish, lima beans

DILL BUTTER
1 teaspoon dried dill weed

Mushrooms, potatoes, carrots, beans, asparagus, spinach, zucchini, fish, chicken, veal

GARLIC BUTTER
1 teaspoon minced fresh garlic

Fish, pasta, bread, grilled meats, spinach, zucchini, cabbage, lima beans

HERBED BUTTER
1 teaspoon powdered mustard
⅛ cup minced fresh parsley
1 tablespoon minced fresh
   shallots
½ teaspoon dried tarragon

Grilled meats, poultry, fish, peas, carrots, celery, green beans

MUSTARD BUTTER
1 ½ teaspoons powdered
   mustard

Ham, pork, cauliflower, broiled salmon and seafood, lentils, lima beans, eggs, greens, sandwiches

NUTMEG BUTTER
1 teaspoon ground nutmeg

Shrimp and seafood, spinach, snap beans, broccoli, brussels sprouts, squash, sweet potatoes, carrots, corn, broiled chicken, peas

PARSLEY BUTTER
½ teaspoon crushed parsley
   flakes

Omelets, clams, white fish, potatoes, carrots, mushrooms, parsnips, corn bread, snails

THYME BUTTER
½ teaspoon dried thyme
   leaves

Fish, chicken, mushrooms, carrots, broiled tomatoes

Herbed
Vinegars &
Oils

THE HERBS & SPICES COOKBOOK

How to Make Herbed Vinegars & Oils

Commercial herbed vinegars and oils really did not become available, or with any selection, until quite recently. Now, there are quite a few brands and quite a good selection. They all have one thing in common. They are quite expensive, and they really do not have to be if you make them yourself.

If you haven't used herbed vinegars before, try them on your salads in place of a usual mayonnaise based salad dressing, or with your favorite oil for an oil and vinegar dressing.

Herbed oils are the ideal thing to rub into beef, pork, poultry, and fish just before cooking, and they can add new flavors to your favorite dishes.

They are quite easy to make and require very little time or effort. Once you make a few, you probably will enjoy making them as gifts. Nowadays, really beautiful art glass bottles are available in many stores (Cost-Plus, Pier One, Crate & Barrel, Pottery Barn, etc.) throughout the United States.

YOU'LL NEED:

Some paper coffee filters or a yard or so of cheesecloth, a plastic funnel, a set of measuring spoons and a measuring cup. If you are going to use the Heating Method, you'll also need a quart-sized pan made of stainless steel, glass or granite-ware. Never, never use aluminum! If you are going to use the Steeping Method, a quart-sized wide mouthed glass jar is required.

The standard wine bottle (750 mm or one quart) is ideal for these oils or vinegars. Or, use those art glass wine/oil bottles that we noted, previously. If you have a dishwasher, put the bottles in the bottom rack, upside down, and wash and dry thoroughly. If you do not use a dishwasher, place the bottles in boiling water for five minutes, and dry carefully to remove all moisture. New corks (hardware stores have them) should be used. Never use used ones. Now, lightly cork the bottles to keep them dry.

THE CHOICE OF VINEGARS IS YOURS:

Types of vinegars include: Red Wine, White Wine, Champagne, Rice, Cider, Malt, and White. In our opinion, the last three are all too strong and not only dominate, but the herbs and spices don' t blend too well with them.

Here, in The California Wine Country we prefer the three wine vinegars: Red, white, and champagne. They are all readily available throughout the United States. Many are probably made in wineries in your home state.

THE CHOICE OF OILS IS YOURS:

Our personal choice is "Lite" Extra Virgin Olive Oil, but you may prefer Corn Oil, Safflower Oil, or Sunflower Oil. All will give you good results. Be sure, however, that the oil you use does not have a strong flavor of its own.

THE CHOICE OF HERBS AND SPICES IS YOURS:

Fresh, dried whole, powdered, flaked, whole ground — whatever form is available where you live — are all acceptable. Be aware, however, that if you grow and dry your own herbs and spices, they are far less potent than the commercial varieties purchased in stores, so you will require more of them.

HEATING OR STEEPING — THE CHOICE IS YOURS:

The Heating Method gives you a finished oil or vinegar immediately. The Steeping Method requires one to four weeks. Both methods are satisfactory, but the Steeping Method will make a superior oil or vinegar when delicate herbs such as basil, cardamom seed, parsley, and thyme are used.

THE HEATING METHOD:
First, place the herbs in the amount noted in a sterilized steeping bottle. Heat the vinegar or oil until it is bubbling, but not boiling, and pour into the bottle, covering the herbs. Cork the bottle and shake vigorously. Let it cool in the steeping bottle.

Next, strain through a paper coffee filter or a doubled cheesecloth into your sterilized bottle. You may want to place fresh or dried sprigs or leaves of the herb in the bottle. Cover it tightly with a new cork, and label it. When cool, it is ready to use.

THE STEEPING METHOD:
Place the herbs in the amounts noted in a sterilized steeping bottle. Pour the desired quantity of vinegar or oil into the bottle, covering the herbs completely. Cork the bottle and shake vigorously. Store for the noted time, shaking when you think of it, every few days.

Strain through a paper coffee filter or a doubled cheesecloth into your sterilized bottle. If you wish, place a fresh or dried sprig or leaves of the herb in the bottle for decor and added flavor. Cork it tightly with a new cork, and label it. You have it, ready to use.

TOO STRONG OR TOO WEAK?

If it is too strong, dilute with the same vinegar or oil that you used. If it is too weak, replace herbs/and or spices with a fresh batch and repeat process.

NOW, ON TO THE RECIPES...

Please Note: We've standardized the recipes to use one pint of the selected vinegar or oil as the base measurement. If you are going to use pint bottles for your final bottling, use the base measurement of one pint (16 ounces/2 cups) for your recipe.

If you are using wine or champagne "splits" (375 ml) bottles, use 12 ounces (1 ½ cups) of the selected vinegar or oil as your base.

If you are using standard wine bottles (750 ml) use 24 ounces (3 cups) of the selected vinegar or oil as your base.

Proportion your herb measurements accordingly.

THE HERBED VINEGARS

BASIL VINEGAR:
1 pint champagne, red wine
  or white wine vinegar
6 fresh basil leaves, or
  ½ ounce dried basil leaves

Place basil in steeping bottle, add hot (not boiling) vinegar, cork and shake. Let cool, strain after about two hours of steeping. This will produce a mild basil vinegar. For a more potent basil vinegar, let it steep for a week, then strain and cork.

Use in tomato dishes like pasta sauces, etc. Good with fish, poultry dishes and salad dressings.

CORIANDER VINEGAR:
1 pint white wine vinegar
2 ounces coriander seeds, or
  1 ounce coriander powder

Crack the coriander seeds with a rolling pin or mortar, and place in steeping bottle with the vinegar. Steep in a warm place for two to three weeks. Strain, pour into bottle, cork and label.

This herbal vinegar will add great flavor to pan fried fish, sausages, frankfurters and hamburgers.

DILL SEED VINEGAR:
1 pint white wine vinegar
1 ounce dried dill seed
2 or 3 dill weed sprigs (optional)

Combine the vinegar with the dill seed in the steeping bottle, and let them steep for five to seven days. Strain and bottle. Add the optional dill weed sprig, if you wish.

Good for potato salads, pasta salads, coleslaw and salad dressings.

DILL WEED VINEGAR:
1 pint white wine vinegar
6 spring or branches fresh dill,
  without seeds, or
  ½ ounce dried dill, without seeds

Place the sprigs of dill in the steeping jar with the vinegar and let it infuse for two weeks. Strain and put into your bottle, with one or two sprigs of the dill. Cork and label.

Dill weed vinegar is quite different from dill seed vinegar. It is quite mild in comparison. Use it for salads, soups and seafood.

FENNEL VINEGAR:
Fennel vinegar is made the same way that dill weed vinegar is made.

Please note that fennel is unusual in the family of herbs and spices in that it tastes like licorice, but it does not impart this taste to other foods. Rather, it enhances the flavor of the foods with which it is used. Try it on cooked vegetables.

GARLIC VINEGAR:
1 pint red wine or white wine vinegar
4 cloves fresh, peeled garlic, bruised
  and coarsely chopped, or
  1 ounce garlic powder or flakes
Pinch of salt (optional)

Place garlic in steeping bottle, add the vinegar, cork and let it steep for two weeks. Shake it once or twice a week. After two weeks, strain and bottle.

Use it for salads and marinades with caution.

LAVENDER VINEGAR:
1 pint white wine vinegar
1 teaspoon dried lavender flowers, or
  2 teaspoons fresh lavender flowers

In a 1-pint jar with lid, combine vinegar and lavender. Cover tightly, shake and set aside overnight. The next day, strain vinegar into a bottle, and discard lavender.

Use it for salad dressings and sauces.

ROSEMARY VINEGAR:
1 pint champagne or white wine vinegar
6 fresh rosemary leaves, or
  1 ounce dried rosemary

Place leaves, then vinegar into steeping bottle, and shake vigorously. Let stand for five to seven days, shaking it daily if possible. Add a whole leaf or a sprig for trim if you wish.

Great for basting beef, lamb and pot roast. Add zest when steaming or boiling new potatoes and cauliflower.

TARRAGON VINEGAR:
1 pint champagne, or white wine vinegar
1 ounce fresh tarragon leaves, or
½ ounce dried tarragon leaves

Heat the vinegar to bubbling, not boiling, and pour over the tarragon which you have placed in the steeping bottle. Cork and let it steep for five to six days, or a week. Strain and place in your final bottle. Some sprigs or leaves of tarragon may be placed in the bottle.

Use for salad dressings, green salads, fish, poultry, and veal. Try it in sauces and in egg dishes.

THE HERBED OILS:

CLOVE & CINNAMON OIL:
2 cups vegetable oil
8 whole cloves
2 cinnamon sticks

Warm the oil on low heat for five minutes. Place cloves and cinnamon in bottle, and pour oil in bottle slowly. Cork and put aside for two weeks.

Use it for sautéing beef and in a beef stew. Also ideal for oiling cake pans and scrambling eggs.

GARLICKY HERB OIL:
1 cup light vegetable oil
1 cup virgin olive oil
1 clove garlic, bruised
1 large or 2 small sprigs fresh tarragon
1 large or 2 small sprigs fresh rosemary

Wash herbs and dry thoroughly. Place in a bottle with garlic. Mix the oils in a pan; heat on low heat for five minutes. Pour warm oil into bottle. Cork tightly and keep two weeks before using.

Before broiling steak or pork chops, brush lightly with this oil.

LEMON CHILI PEPPER OIL:
2 cups virgin olive oil
Peel of 1 lemon in a long, narrow strip
Your choice of any two red
  chili peppers, fresh or dried.

Place lemon, peppers and oil in steeping bottle, cover with cheesecloth, place in sunny spot for a week or 10 days, and stir every day or so.

Ideal for green salads, broiling chicken, and fish.

SPICY OIL:
2 cups light vegetable oil
3 whole cloves
3 whole allspice berries
2 cinnamon sticks
1 tablespoon coriander seeds
6 cardamom pods, crushed
10 whole black peppercorns
Peel of half a lemon

Warm the oil in a pan over low heat for five minutes, remove from stove, and add all ingredients. Stir gently, and put into bottle. Cork tightly and wait two weeks before using.

Use this oil for salads, over pasta, or to brown any meat.

Herb and Spice Mixes

It's very convenient to have a selection of blends of herbs and spices, and there are many available in most supermarkets. However, many contain herbs, spices, or salt that you really don't like, or shouldn't have for reasons of health.

Here are some recipes for you to use as they are written; but we urge you to create your own to fit your particular tastes and requirements.

They can, properly used, enhance a simple stew, meatloaf, soup or roast to a new culinary height.

BOUQUET GARNI:
1-2 bay leaves
1-2 sprigs fresh thyme
1-2 sprigs fresh rosemary
1-2 sprigs fresh parsley
1-2 sprigs fresh basil

Tie herbs sprigs together into a bundle for easy removal before serving or finishing a dish. The number of sprigs you use is determined by the size of pot and quantity of food to be cooked.

CHILI POWDER (Salt-free):
6 dried hot chilies, 2 to 4 inches
1 ½ teaspoons dried cumin seeds
2 teaspoons dried oregano
1 teaspoon sweet paprika
½ teaspoon garlic powder (optional)

Grind all ingredients in spice mill until they are very fine. Makes about ⅓ cup.

CRAB-BOIL SPICES:
¼ cup pickling spices (see recipe on
    Page 233)
2 tablespoons mustard seeds
2 tablespoons whole black
    peppercorns
1 tablespoon celery seeds
2 tablespoons dried hot red pepper
    flakes
2 teaspoons ground ginger
5 bay leaves
2 teaspoons dried oregano
1 tablespoon minced dried chives
¼ cup sea salt

Combine all ingredients and stir until
they form a coarse powder. It will
keep in a tightly-sealed container for
several months in a cool, dark place.

CURRY POWDER:
This is a basic recipe for a curry
powder. Make just a little bit and try
it. For example, if you want it milder,
use less white pepper, red pepper
and ground ginger. It you want it
hotter, just increase them.

1 teaspoon ground allspice
4 teaspoons ground coriander
1 teaspoon cumin seeds
1 teaspoon fenugreek seeds
½ teaspoon ground ginger
1 teaspoon dry mustard
¼ teaspoon red pepper flakes
½ teaspoon ground white pepper
3 teaspoons ground turmeric

Grind and mix spices carefully. Sauté
in a little butter or margarine over low
heat for 1 to 2 minutes to release the
flavors.

HERBES DE PROVENCE MIX:
An assortment of dried herbs most commonly used in Southern French cooking. This is a blend that can be used to season meat, poultry and vegetables.

2 tablespoons dried basil
2 tablespoons dried rosemary
2 tablespoons dried thyme
1 tablespoons dried marjoram
1 teaspoon ground fennel
1 teaspoon rubbed or dried sage
1 teaspoon dried lavender

Combine in a blender and mix until well blended. Bottle to keep fresh.

ITALIAN HERB BLEND:
2 tablespoons ground basil
2 teaspoons ground marjoram
1 teaspoon ground oregano
1 clove garlic, minced
1 tablespoon minced onion

Blend thoroughly and, if not used at once, store in an airtight container.

MEDITERRANEAN BLEND:
1 teaspoon ground coriander
1 teaspoon ground cumin
1 teaspoon garlic powder
1 teaspoon onion powder
1 teaspoon oregano leaves
¼ teaspoon ground red pepper
½ teaspoon thyme leaves

Crush oregano and thyme leaves. Mix with remaining ingredients.

MEXICAN BLEND:
½ teaspoon chili powder
1 teaspoon cilantro
½ teaspoon ground coriander
1 teaspoon ground cumin
1 teaspoon onion powder
½ teaspoon red pepper

Blend all ingredients together and store in an airtight container.

PICKLING SPICES BLEND:
2 tablespoons mustard seed
1 tablespoon whole allspice
2 teaspoons coriander seeds
2 whole cloves
1 teaspoon ground ginger
1 teaspoon dried red pepper flakes
1 bay leaf, crumbled
1 cinnamon stick

Blend all ingredients together and store in an airtight container.

THAI SPICE BLEND:
⅛ teaspoon ground cinnamon
1 teaspoon ground coriander
½ teaspoon ground cumin
½ teaspoon garlic powder
½ teaspoon ground ginger
½ teaspoon onion powder
¼ teaspoon ground red pepper

Blend all ingredients together and store in an airtight container.

Index

A

A Classic Chili 123
African Squash Soup 61
Angel-Hair Pasta Sautéed and Cooked in Fish Stock with Lobster . . 150
Apple Chutney 214
Artichokes Stuffed with Smoldering Shrimp 75

B

Baby Lettuce Salad with Prawns and Grapefruit 80
Baked Chèvre Salad with Fuji Apples and Toasted Pecans 78
Baked Cranberry Pork Chops 116
Baked Peaches with Warm Raspberry Compote 183
Baked Sweet Potatoes with Apples 170
Barbecued Happy Duck 140
Basil Pita Triangles with Hummus and Red Pepper 46
Basil Pork Chops Barbera 117
Basil Vinegar 225
Biscotti 196
Black Bean Chili 64
Black Bean Salsa Dip 41
Black Bean-Corn Salsa 204
Black Forest Brownies 197
Blackberry-Mint Butter 215
Blue Cheese Onion Pie 47
Bouquet Garni 230
Bow Tie Pasta with Chicken, Mushrooms and Artichokes 90
Braised Beef Ragout with Sage Pappardelle and
    Roasted Garlic Cabernet Sauce 112
Braised Rabbit with Sweet Potatoes, Lentils, and
    Meyer Lemon, Garlic and Green Beans 120
Brandied Bananas 196
Brandied Cranberry Apple Relish 213
Brandied Peach and Plum Soup 61
Broccoli with Hazelnuts 175
Butternut Squash Pancake with Baked Garlic Cream and
    Smoked Salmon 35

C

Cajun Spice Butter 216
California Brandied Fruit Cake 188
California Fish Soup 161
California Rice 103
Caramel Apple Tart 193
Caramel Lavender Ice Cream 184
Caramel Surprise Apple Pie 181
Carneros Lamb 125
Cheddar-Herb Scones 44
Cheese Tortellini with a Pesto Cream Sauce and Grilled Chicken . . . 96
Chicken Bulgur Salad 79
Chicken Cantaloupe Salad with Ginger Dressing 85
Chicken Curry 138
Chicken Scallops with Tomato, Oakleaf Lettuce and Fresh Basil . . . 139
Chicken Waldorf Salad 72
Chicken with Prawns 132

Chile Banana Salsa 203
Chili Powder 230
Chocolate Bread Pudding 192
Chocolate Chip Pumpkin Pie 194
Chocolate Lavender Truffles 184
Chocolate Pumpkin Cake 185
Cilantro Cured Salmon 154
Cilantro Salmon Tostada 34
Cilantro Sauce 206
Cinnamon Chocolate Pecan Pie 179
Classic Salsa 205
Clove & Cinnamon Oil 228
Cold Cucumber Soup with Dill 55
Coriander Vinegar 225
Crab-Boil Spices 231
Cranberry Chile Salsa 203
Cream of Carrot Soup with Dill 58
Curried Carrot Soup 54
Curried Chicken and Olive Soup 60
Curried Chicken in Cracker Bread 39
Curried Chicken Salad 84
Curry Powder 231
Custard-Rhubarb Pie 199

D
Dill Seed Vinegar 226
Dill Weed Vinegar 226
Dried Fruit Chutney 214

E
Easy Three Bean Salad 84
Eggplant Soup 63
Estofado 111

F
Fennel Vinegar 226
Fettuccini in Basil Cream 89
Fettuccini with Lemon Caper Sauce 99
Fettuccini with Sun-Dried Tomatoes, California Prunes and Mustard . 93
Four Cheeses Cheesecake 40
Fresh Basil and Tomatoes Pasta 92
Fresh Corn Chowder 57
Fresh Thyme and Tomato Sorbet 198
Fricassee of Rabbit with Wild Mushrooms 121
Fusilli Pasta with Shrimp Salad 83

G
Garlic Mashed Potatoes 168
Garlic Vinegar 227
Garlicky Herb Oil 228
Ginger Apple Tart 191
Ginger Pear Tart 192
Ginger Pumpkin Soup 53
Green Olivado 43
Green Pasta with Herbs 92
Grilled Butterflied Leg of Lamb 107

Grilled Chicken Breast with Black Bean and Roasted Corn Salsa . . 137
Grilled Cornish Game Hen Salad with Orange-Mint Dressing 143
Grilled Scallop Salad with Basil Vinaigrette Dressing 76
Grilled Steak Provencal 114

H
Harvest Apple Cake 186
Harvest Stew 124
Hazelnut Crusted Salmon with Spicy Peach Sauce 149
Herb Baked Salmon with Lobster Lemon Thyme Cream Sauce 156
Herb Marinated Lamb Chops 127
Herbed Garlic Butter 216
Herbed Quesadillas 32
Herbes De Provence Mix 232
Hot Tomato Sauce 211

I
Italian Gorgonzola Cheesecake 36
Italian Herb Blend 232
Italian Rice Torta 102

J
Jamaican Red Bean Soup 65

L
Lamb with Cilantro-Cumin Crust 109
Lavender Roasted Cornish Hens 144
Lavender Roasted Red Potatoes 169
Lavender Vinegar 227
Lemon Chili Pepper Oil 229
Lemon Curd Tart with Hazelnut Crust,
    Fresh Strawberries and Raspberries 195
Linguini with Clams Monterey 100
Linguini with Shrimp and Pesto 151
Loin of Pork Patties with Blackberry Salsa 126

M
Medallions of Salmon with Pine Nut Herb Crust 153
Mediterranean Blend 232
Mediterranean Green Beans 171
Mediterranean Medley 208
Mediterranean Pasta Salad 82
Mexican Blend 233
Mint Glazed Carrots 176
Minted Grilled Lamb 108
Minted Red Onion Blackberry Relish 213
Mixed Lettuce Greens with Basil Oil and Blue Cheese 74
Mushroom Beef Stew 110
Mushroom Cream Sauce with Tarragon 207
Mushroom-Pepper Chicken 136

N
Noodles with Minted Cucumber Sauce 99
Nutmeg-Onion Potato Bake 168

O

Onions in Chardonnay Cream 171
Orange Pecan Chicken Salad 77
Oven-Dried Tomato Salad with Herb Dressing 70
Oven-Roasted Salmon with an Orange and Dill Beurre Blanc 155

P

Pappardelle with Sweet Red Peppers 95
Parsley Creamed Carrots 172
Pasta Salad with Sesame Dressing 71
Pasta with Scallops in Lemon Herb Cream Sauce 94
Peach N' Pineapple Salsa 204
Pear Gingerbread Upside Down Cake 189
Pearl Onion Compote 212
Peppered Salmon with Lavender 157
Peppernut Cookies 191
Persimmon Walnut Cake with Champagne Sea Foam Sauce 187
Picante Red Wine Sauce 211
Pickling Spices Blend 233
Poached Figs over Ice Cream 190
Poached Pears in Zinfandel 190
Polenta with Italian Sausage 102
Potato and Butternut Squash Gratin with
    Caramelized Onions and Fresh Thyme 167
Potato-Parsnip Pancakes with Smoked Salmon,
    Lemon Sour Cream and Fresh Dill 38
Pumpkin Ice Cream Pie 180
Pumpkin Soup with Apples and Black Walnuts 53

R

Raspberry Rose Salad 83
Red Bell Pepper Soup 59
Red Onion Marmalade 212
Red Potato Salad 85
Ricotta Cheese-Lemon Thyme Tart with Sweet Cornmeal Crust . . . 182
Roast Chicken with Pine Nut Dressing 134
Roast Leg of Lamb with Pesto Pine Nut Filling 119
Roasted Cornish Game Hens with Pecan-Date Stuffing 142
Roasted Rack of Lamb with Cabernet Rosemary Tangerine Sauce . 118
Roasted Red Potatoes with Garlic and Thyme 169
Rosemary Vinegar 227

S

Saffron Risotto 98
Salmon Bisque 54
Salsa Carib 206
Salsa Santa Fe 205
Sautéed Chicken & Grapes In a Creamy Gingered Wine Sauce . . . 131
Sautéed Cucumbers 175
Sautéed Medallions of Tuna with Papaya Salsa and Cilantro Pesto . 159
Savory Focaccia 43
Savory Stilton Cheese Tart 33
Scallop Sauté with Leek and Allspice 158
Sea Bass Fillets Baked in Herbed-Wine 163
Sea-Bass Baked with Fennel 152
Seafood and Kielbasa Sausage Gumbo 160
Seared Venison Tartar with Pink Peppercorn Crust
    and Pickled Beets 45

Shanghai Lobster Risotto with Spicy Ginger and
   Julienne of Green Onions 162
Sherried Crab Soup 51
Shrimp & Citrus Salad with Curry Dressing 69
Smoked Salmon Puffs 47
Southern Green Beans 176
Spaghetti al Fromaggio 98
Spaghetti Primavera 101
Spiced Carrots 172
Spiced Red Cabbage 173
Spiced Roasted Garlic Cloves 170
Spicy Black Bean Salad 72
Spicy Broccoli 173
Spicy Cherry Sauce 210
Spicy Chocolate Macaroons 197
Spicy Herbed Nuts 42
Spicy Oil 229
Spicy Plum Pork 127
Spicy Sesame Sticks 42
Spicy Tangine of Lamb with Apples 122
Strawberry-Rhubarb Crisp 199

T
Tandoori-Style Roast Chicken 135
Tarragon Chicken Breast Chardonnay 133
Tarragon Vinegar 228
Thai Chicken Salad 73
Thai Spice Blend 233
Tomato Provencal Soup 62
Tomato Soup Fumé 52
Tomato-Zucchini Bake 174
Tortilla Soup 56
Turkey Meatballs with Ginger Chutney 145
Turkey Picadillo 141

V
Vegetable Ragout 174
Vintner's Stew 115

W
Walnut-Mustard Butter 215
Warm Mushroom Salad with Champagne Vinaigrette and
   Goat Cheese Croutons 81
Wild Mushroom Ravioli with White Truffle Oil 91
Wild Mushroom Sauce with Rosemary and Bacon 209
Wild Mushroom Tarts 31

Y
Yogurt Mustard Chicken 144

Z
Zinfandel Noodles 97
Zinfandel Peppercorn Sauce 210
Zucchini Blossom Fritters with Avocado Mousse and
   Smoked Tomato Sauce 37

Postscript

If your book, gift, or gourmet store does not have these books you may order them by phone, fax, e-mail or mail. Your money back if you are not delighted.

"The California Wine Country Cookbook II", a collection of 172 favorite recipes by 102 chefs of "The California Wine Country." There's a section on cooking with wine and a brief history of wine in California . . . . $12.95 plus $3.00 S&H

"The California Wine Country Herbs & Spices Cookbook, The Revised Second Edition ", a collection of 212 recipes by 96 chefs, winemakers, and wineries, featuring herbs and spices. Included in this book are recipes for making herbed oils and vinegars, and your own spice mixes . . . . $14.95 plus $3.00 S&H

"The Great Little Food With Wine Cookbook," 76 cooking with wine recipes, pairing wine with food, how and where to buy wine, ordering wine in a restaurant, and much more. Every recipe has a wine selection, pairing your own recipes with wine, deciphering wine bottle labels, what glassware you really need, and a simple and easy-to-remember explanation of American wines and what foods go with them . . . . $7.95 plus $2.00 S&H

"Cooking With Wine" 86 winery chefs share 172 of their favorite recipes for cooking with wine and pairing wine with food. There is a description of American wines and their pairing with many different foods . . . . $14.95 plus $3.00 S&H

"Salsas!" A collection of 86 exciting salsa recipes from Cuba, the Caribbean Islands, Africa, Latin America, the Far East , Spain and Portugal, with beverage recipes . . . . $6.95 plus $2.00 S&H

TO ORDER

By phone, call toll free 24 hours, 7 days a week (800) 852-4890 with your American Express, Discover, MasterCard, or Visa credit card.

By fax, 24 hours, 7 days a week, (707) 538-7371 with your American Express, Discover, MasterCard, or Visa credit card number, expiration date, and signature.

By e-mail, <Hoffpress@worldnet.att.net> with your credit card number and expiration date.

By mail, send your check, money order, or credit card information to: The Hoffman Press, P.O. Box 2996 Santa Rosa, CA 95405.

The End

THE HERBS & SPICES COOKBOOK